THANKS FOR ASKING, MR. PRESIDENT

by

Caroline Hastings Babington

Published by
R & E PUBLISHERS
P. O. Box 2008
Saratoga, California 95070

Library of Congress Cataloging-in-Publication Data

Babington, Caroline Hastings, 1919-
Thanks for asking, Mr. President.

Bibliography: p.
1. United States--Economic conditions--1945-
2. United States--Social conditions--1945-
I. Title.
HC106.5.B25 1986 330.973'092 86-10006
ISBN 0-88247-754-4

My sincere appreciation to Pat Piell for her patience and cooperation in typing this manuscript

TO ALL MY COUNTRYMEN

Table Of Contents

Introduction

When President Ronald Reagan announced his proposed economic program to bring our nation back to a state of sound fiscal management, he also said that if anyone had a better solution than the one he was recommending, they should speak up and he would be willing to listen. This set me to thinking as to how this great country might achieve Mr. Reagan's goal of a balanced budget and at the same time, allow for all of its people to have their basic needs supplied and enough money to enjoy those leisure time pursuits so necessary to their individual fulfillment. There must be a way for all to live with peace and happiness, secure in the knowledge that no great catastrophe would befall them – at least none that could not be overcome.

I started out by defining the problems that now exist in our nation as a whole. Not all of our people are faced with all of these problems but there are some areas of concern that, whether we admit it or not, do affect the entire population: the threat of a nuclear war, pollution, shortages of vital natural resources, and a failing economy. Other matters affect some people at different times in their lives but are always a source of uncertainty for one never knows when he may be a victim of such misfortune. Next, I endeavored to find solutions to the existing problems, bearing in mind the need to resolve these concerns in accord with the philosophy of the greatest good for the greatest number of our people.

This, then, is my answer to President Reagan's challenge: a way to restore the hope of our nation for a future in which ALL WILL BE WELL.

Chapter One
It All Begins With The Individual

We find ourselves in a world today that is sadly lacking in those things that are so necessary to our survival.

Throughout history man has encountered some degree of human suffering and it was usually caused by his inhuman treatment of his fellow man or his disregard for his environment.

There has always been an adequate supply of the resources needed for man to exist on this planet and there still is an abundance. Our present dilemma has been brought about by our misuse of these commodities and the unwillingness of countries to share those things that are native to their terrain.

No state, nation, or country owns the national resources found within its geographical area. They have no right to lay claim to what is not theirs, but, rather, a God-given gift to all of the inhabitants of the Earth. It is just their greed and refusal to share with others that has brought our world to its present deplorable state. There is no need to stockpile; to curtail production; or to charge exorbitant prices while others suffer from a lack of those vital commodities so important to their well-being and, at times, their very survival. This is not to say that remuneration should not be made for goods received. There must be some incentive to produce. But it does mean that a way must be found for a fair and equitable distribution of these essential commodities.

We will never know peace on this Earth while human suffering prevails.

We can only begin to understand our national and international problems by being cognizant of the fact that the conditions that plague the world are the same as those that we, as individuals, are faced with in our daily lives. Each day we awaken to the challenge of how we are going to meet the needs of ourselves, our families, and any other members of our community for whom we have a responsibility. To do so, we utilize whatever available resources are in easy reach. We first tackle the problem of overcoming the night's fast and prepare, or have prepared for us, our first meal of the day. This can be likened to a country's need to feed all of its inhabitants on an ongoing basis. If we do not have ample food with which to start our day, we are not going to be able to function to the best of our ability. We will be inclined to be a bit lethargic, probably somewhat out of sorts, and unable to deal effectively with matters that present themselves to us for our consideration or action. We will be inclined to devote an excessive amount of time and energy to thinking about our hunger and seeking ways to overcome the situation. This problem, whether we admit it or not, will be foremost in our minds. And so it will be with the masses of people in those areas of the world where there is not an adequate supply of food. To be ready to meet life's challenges, we must first provide for our own basic needs.

The lack of sufficient amount of food will always create problems for any individual or country. It will also be the cause for some action to be taken. On an individual basis, we will have to decide what course to follow. All will be well if we have the funds necessary to purchase some food and an available source of supply. Lacking either of these, the problem becomes more acute and can set up a whole new chain of events. It is not a situation that can be overcome by bureaucratic red tape. We want immediate results and may have to resort to illegal action to achieve success. This is a risk that many have taken. No man is going to sit back and go hungry, or watch his loved ones suffer from malnutrition without making some effort to provide a solution. If stealing is the only way open to him, then this is what he will do. He may be willing to trade his services or barter for food, but our lifestyle does not always allow for this means of exchange. It is a sad situation when a human being must break laws, risk his integrity, and forever be labeled a criminal because he had to resort to this means to obtain food. Our society has allowed this to become the plight of many and then punished these individuals because adequate provisions had not been made to allow them the opportunity to provide for their own needs with dignity; to meet each day's challenges in keeping with their ability to perform at their peak; rather than being reduced to malcontent individuals.

If man is not allowed to meet his own requirements for maintaining himself on a day-to-day basis, he is going to have serious problems with his life. If countries are unable to provide for their people, then they, too, will have problems on a larger scale. Wars have been started because of a country's inability to maintain itself, or because of the anger of the masses at being denied the means to survive. We must begin to deal with individuals, to be cognizant of their problems, and to establish solutions as a way to circumvent problems with the vast majorities.

It is a noble gesture to provide food stamps for the needy, but our present system does not involve all who are eligible to receive this aid. Many people are too proud to ask for what they consider charity, others are not aware that they qualify for the existing program. We must devise a plan that will include all of our citizens who are in need of this type of assistance. The number of unemployed persons residing in each household would be a contributing factor in such a determination. The combined income of the employed individuals, as reported for income tax purposes, would be divided by the number of dependents and food stamps then automatically issued to those families or individuals who qualify by virtue of their economic need. The person designated as "head of household" should be the recipient. The purchasing power of these stamps would not include non-essential items; e.g., any form of tobacco, alcohol, or non-nutritional snack foods. Guidelines for their use would, of necessity, be established and enforced.

So now all of our citizens, upon arising in the morning, will be able to start their day without any thought as to how they are going to meet their nutritional needs. They can turn their attention to the next item on the agenda. This may be getting to their place of employment on time. We all live by our clocks and our lives would be somewhat disoriented if we did not follow the patterns established by our twenty-four hour cycles.

For most people, getting to and from work requires transportation. Few are lucky enough to be able to walk to their place of employment. We are a wheel-oriented culture. Without the invention of the wheel, which made its appearance in the Bronze Age somewhere between 3500 and 1000 B.C., we would still be living in what we now term the "Dark Ages"; a period in medieval times known for its intellectual stagnation. Automobiles are almost as vital to our well-being as is our need for food. We spend as much money on these two purchases as we do on all of our other combined expenditures. We cannot visualize a lifestyle without some form of door-to-door transportation. Lately, we have been encountering difficulty in maintaining our automobiles on a functioning basis due to the high cost and, at times, lack of availability of gas and oil that we have not previously deemed possible. There seems little hope of our being able to rectify this situation in the foreseeable future.

The oil producing countries of the Middle East are enjoying their role as "Controllers" of an oil supply that is needed by the rest of the world. They threaten to reduce production, to increase prices, to sell only for gold, and we must do our best to avoid any disharmony that will cause them to refuse to sell us any of their precious commodity at any price. And so we live in a state of apprehension. Will there be enough oil available so that we can continue to live in the manner to which we have become accustomed and, even if it is available, will we be able to purchase a sufficient amount to meet our needs?

As individuals we are concerned about what we can do to overcome this plight. Actually, there seems to be very little that we can do other than curtailing the use of our cars whenever possible. But this causes us some dissatisfaction, as well as inconvenience. We become irritated by these circumstances over which we have no control. And so the masses seek to place the blame on government officials who they feel have not been effectively performing their duties to their constituents. Thus, the problem is now not an individual concern, but a national concern that has the potential for becoming an international disaster.

Rather than stepping up our defense programs and engaging in threats to end diplomatic or economic relationships with these offending countries, we would be wise to establish a system of barter to exchange goods for goods. Price should not be a factor. If each country would maximize production of those things that are unique to its geographical area and exchange their products for those that they are unable to produce, there would be little need to worry about monetary matters.

A world organization, such as the United Nations, could be responsible for monitoring the exchange of goods. Such a system would be based on need as determined by population. Each country would be responsible for submitting an inventory of the commodities they require, as well as the amount needed. Acceptance of these statistics would be based on their current population count. Allotments would thus be fair and equitable for all. In order for any country to be granted their request for goods, they would have to export a pre-determined amount of their available natural resources. A central accounting center would be needed to keep a record of the transfer of goods between countries and to function as a World Bank to record credits and debits. Credit would be given to each country for exports made, which could then be drawn against as goods were imported. The accounts might not always balance. Credits could be built up against a time of natural disaster that might lessen a country's ability to produce. Advances in credit would be allowed if a real need presented itself. Approval for such advances would be studied and determined by a panel of experts in the area of concern. There would not be any distribution of products for use in making any type of war-related armaments. All goods would be used to benefit man, not to destroy him. This would put an end to the production of those things which are a vast waste of our natural resources. It would also put an end to any country's ability to dominate the world, or to threaten the economy of those who are dependent upon its resources. A World Bank would solve such problems.

Now that we have dealt with the problem of overcoming any further fuel crisis, we will turn our attention to another area of concern in our daily lives. We may have ample food, adequate transportation, but find ourselves in ill health, unable to enjoy and reap the rewards of our newfound blessings. Few people enjoy a lifetime totally free of the need for medical assistance. We have reached a point in our society where medical costs are almost prohibitive to the average citizen. Now only the wealthy can enjoy the finest of care in the best facilities.

To be financially responsible for the health of one's family is a very grave concern. One incident can wipe out a life savings. It is better to be a charity case than to be mildly affluent. Medical insurance is available and it is a blessing for those who can afford to take advantage of it, or who have access to this type of coverage through their place of employment. But too often, ill health is a financial as well as a physical problem and coping with the physical aspect is all that a person should have to endure.

Private citizens should not be required to bear the cost of malpractice insurance that members of the medical profession have deemed necessary for their survival. Nor should they have to pay for the costs involved in unnecessary hospital expenses brought about by mismanagement of the facilities and over-expansion in areas that have not been proven necessary to the overall care of the patients. It is a sad situation when a person in need of medical assistance has to be so burdened with these additional fees. All of this adds to the dissatisfaction of a vast majority of our citizens. The end result is disenchantment with a government that is unable to provide for the well-being of its populace.

We are all familiar with "socialized medicine" in England and have heard the pros and cons of its effectiveness. It may have flaws to be ironed out, but it is a step in the right direction. The British National Health Service was established in 1948 and when even its most ardent supporters concede that it has some major shortcomings, opinion polls consistently show public approval of the plan to be overwhelming. Even the physicians who have been the strongest and most persistent critics of the plan do not appose it in principle. "No one in Britain is afraid to be sick because of the cost of care. The quality of acute care in Britain is generally acknowledged to be high and the British seem to have done a relatively good job of ensuring patient access to the health care system via a large corps of general practioners."[1] So while we may not want to follow their methods, the British have proven the value of providing every citizen with adequate medical care without regard to his financial means.

In our country this could be achieved by instituting a health care program, based on a system of checks and balances, relating to need and services available. Every physician would be responsible for a given number of patients; in return for which, he would receive remuneration for services rendered. This is much like our Medicaid program; however, once the plan becomes instituted, reimbursement for services would be on a patient basis rather than on a service rendered basis. This may seem to be somewhat unfair because some areas of medicine require special schooling and more expertise. Why shouldn't a specialist receive more money than a general practitioner? However, those who choose the medical profession as their career in life should have enough interest in helping others to be willing to do so without expecting to become wealthy from these services. The human body is not to be considered something that can be capitalized on because of greed.

To be a doctor is to be a servant to one's fellow man, not a god to be placed on a pedestal and revered. There are many fine men in the medical profession who have a real concern for their patients, but there are also many who enter into the profession because they see it as being very lucrative. They set themselves up not to serve others but to earn unnecessarily exorbitant fees. These are the people that the medical profession could well do without. These are the people who would eliminate themselves from this line of work were they to be granted a standard fee for all services rendered, that would be the same for all doctors, regardless of their area of specialization. These same standards should also be set for the dental profession. The amount of money that doctors earn should provide them with the ability to meet all of their needs for food, clothing, shelter, transportation, and recreation. The need to accumulate vast amounts of wealth should not be their motivating force.

We try to accumulate wealth in order to fulfill our desire for material possessions, expensive recreation, an education for ourselves or our offspring, and so that we can provide for all of our creature comforts in our retirment years. If we have no need to set aside funds for these purposes, we could utilize our earnings for our daily living and our need to acquire large sums of money would be lessened.

Material possessions are important only when they fill a need. To acquire more than we can use will not contribute to the enjoyment of life.

Some forms of expensive recreation are worthwhile – travel, the theater, celebrations for special occasions; but for the most part, we can be content with the company of friends, the resources provided by nature, participation in sports and games, and in the pursuit of our own innate desire to be creative.

Education should be granted to all on an equal basis and the cost should be nominal. The school taxes imposed on individuals are all that should be required to guarantee every person an education in keeping with his ability and desire to learn.

Our elderly citizens should be able to enjoy their declining years without any thought as to where they are going to find the monies necessary to do so. Our present Social Security system should be revised to include all of our senior citizens and to provide them with adequate funds for food, clothing, shelter, recreation, and the ability to make purchases on their own.

Now with all of these concerns put to rest, each day can be lived to the fullest, free of worry and the need to expend energy in useless areas of endeavor. We can rise and shine, enjoy our breakfast, tackle the day's chores, and then be at liberty to pursue those activities that are of interest to us. We can go to bed without concern for tomorrow for we know that all will be well. Some adversity may befall us, but it will never be devastating. A solution will always be available and assistance will be provided in keeping with our needs.

If every individual can face life with the confidence needed to keep him feeling secure, the problems of the country, as a whole, will begin to dissipate. Where there is no hunger, no untreated illness, no lack of those commodities that supply our basic needs for adequate shelter and creature comforts, there will be no need to rise up and demand, by forceful means, that these needs be supplied.

And so, as we continue to live happily ever after, our national government can concern itself solely with the programs that provide for the well-being of the populace and forego those that in no way contribute to human needs. As long as all of our citizens are supplied with those things so important to their survival and the enjoyment of life, there will be no reason for our elected officials to do anything other than take measures to continue this ideal state. We will all live with peace in the knowledge that cooperation between nations exist, as we share in the natural resources of each other's terrain. The need for national defense will cease to exist. A new beginning will emerge for all the people of our country.

Footnotes

[1]*Science*, July 21, 1978. American Association For The Advancement of Science, British National Health Service, pps. 239-241.

Chapter Two
Human Dignity

Once we have achieved a state of peaceful existence for all of our citizens by making adequate food, clothing, shelter, recreational facilities, medical care, educational advantages, and security in their retirement years available to them, we must still take into consideration the need for each individual to achieve maximum self-respect and self-motivation. It is not wise to hand out all of these essentials without giving any thought to the recipient's participation in assuming responsibility for his own welfare. Every adult should be required to make a contribution, in accordance with his ability, to his overall plan for his survival.

It is important to one's self-esteem to be engaged in an activity that is enjoyable, as well as usefull. It is demeaning to hand out alms to a person who is able-bodied and capable.

Our present welfare system is a perfect example of infringement on human dignity. There are some cases where it serves a purpose without taking away from an individual's feeling of self-worth, but these are in the minority. Far too many people on welfare are capable of performing some useful task that would benefit themselves and others. This lack of self-actualization can only breed discontent. Even those who claim to be delighted with their situation are not really as satisfied as they would be if they were actively engaged in a self-fulfilling occupation for which they were adequately reimbursed.

Welfare payments are necessary when there are a number of young children, who require ongoing care, in a household that is not provided for by a gainfully employed person. This situation usually occurs when the mother is the only adult member in the family. They are also necessary as a stopgap measure to aid in times of illness or loss of position on the part of the breadwinner. Such circumstances will generally be short term and, therefore, should be re-evaluated on a monthly basis. This will entail some bureaucratic red tape, but it will be less expensive to the taxpayers than continuing unnecessary welfare payments. A system of checks and balances must be maintained for the benefit of all concerned.

Three months should be the maximum time for any able-bodied person, who is not faced with debilitating conditions. to receive welfare payments. If he is unable to secure employment by his own efforts, he should be assigned to a job and required to assume responsibility for himself and his dependents. The gravy train is long overdue. Those who are on it must be made to find other ways to reach their destination. We cannot continue to give a free ride without setting limits for its termination. To do so is unfair to the persons involved and to the taxpayers who must bear the burden of the unnecessary expense.

Unemployment compensation, like welfare payments, should only be used as a temporary measure. Once again, three months should be the maximum time for benefits to be paid to any individual. Jobs should be made available for those who are unable to find employment on their own and for people who are waiting to return to their established place of employment when the need for their services is restored. If a person's work suspension exceeds the established three months payment period, he should not be subsidized for the entire time that he is laid off. Remuneration for assigned jobs should be on a scale equal to that paid under the Unemployment Compensation Act.

To assure a sufficient number of jobs for all of our potential working force, local communities, states, and the federal government should establish a variety of work programs geared to the improvement of substandard living conditions; the preservation of the environment; and the production of food for the purpose of increasing the overall supply and thus decreasing the cost to the consumer. The latter might be accomplished through the cultivation of farms and the subsequent processing, canning, and packaging of the crops grown. Some of the money that is now allocated for unemployment compensation and welfare payments could be redirected to use for these purposes. Eventually some of the programs would become self-sufficient.

When assigning an individual to a job, consideration must be given to his innate ability. It is the only way that we can maximize human potential. We all function at our best when we are allowed to pursue those activities that we enjoy and that we do well. To try to force a person to perform tasks that are not to his liking or for which he does not have the necessary qualifications is to try to put a square peg in a round hole. It is impossible to meet with any degree of success. Those who perform menial tasks should be regarded with the same respect as the industrial giants, professional people, and the political leaders of our country. Every man deserves to be held in esteem for what he is capable of doing as a functioning member of society. Some have more responsible positions, but that does not make them better, in any way, than their fellow man.

Race, creed, age, sex, or national origin should never be a factor in job placement.

In order to determine each person's interest and field of endeavor for which he is best suited, a vocational interest test should be given to all as a part of our educational system. Some will be many faceted and capable of working at a variety of different occupations; others will prefer to stay with one type of employment for a lifetime. These differences should be taken into consideration by a job placement service that is available to every individual upon completion of his education.

We often feel locked into our present environment because of the fear of not being able to find suitable employment in another part of the country and/or of losing our accrued employee benefits, if we leave our current position. This could be overcome by establishing one central office for job placement in each geographical area. A person desiring to relocate would merely make application for a positon, in keeping with his capabilities, to the job placement bureau in the location of his choice. Credit for payments made for life insurance, retirement plans, and group medical policies would follow an individual as he moved about in a job situation. No man should be a slave to his fringe benefits. All this could easily be accomplished with the use of our sophisticated computer technology. It would allow for variety in one's life experience even though he chose to remain in one type of employment.

Not everyone is going to be employed away from his home, nor will everyone want to be. Many occupations and trades can be carried out at one's place of residence. People thus engaged comprise the large number of individuals whom we categorize as self-employed. They make their contribution to society without accruing any of the fringe benefits enjoyed by those who are employed by outside organizations. However, they have the same need for unemployment, health, and retirement benefits. They should be allowed to participate in the unemployment compensation program and have group health and retirement plans available to them. A viable health insurance plan and an all-encompassing social security program would meet their needs, but until such time as these measures have become a reality, other solutions will have to be provided.

We will all begin to feel more relaxed with our financial situation as some additional security factors are made available. However, we will still have a need for sound fiscal planning on the part of the government. Prices must not be allowed to run rampant. No man should make an exorbitant profit if in doing so he is depriving others of goods that are necessary to their survival. Some control must be exercised so that every man will have the ability to purchase the essentials to his well-being and still have money for recreation and pleasurable items. Prices for commodities should be established, with a range of flexibility to allow for competition and the kind and amount of service that goes into their distribution. Wage scales should be set based on the degree of difficulty of a position, as well as the amount of responsibility involved. In either case, maximum and minimum guidelines should be maintained.

Rare or non-essential items need not be subject to price control. We cannot put a price on a great masterpiece or a rare gemstone. Collectors, themselves, will determine the value of these artifacts. They will always be decided by the wealth of the highest bidder.

Every individual has a built-in desire to prove his worth. He can only do so by being productive in some area and by receiving recognition for his efforts in the form of financial remuneration or approval from his fellow man. A great artist or composer may not receive any monetary reimbursement for his works, but to have them accepted and acclaimed is satisfaction in itself. This type of self-actualization is important to one's mental health and cannot be overlooked as being necessary to personal integrity. For this reason, every individual must be allowed to contribute, in some way, to his own feeling of importance. We must not do anything to deprive him of this opportunity. In the event that a person becomes disabled and is, therefore, unable to maintain himself through his usual means of gainful employment, he should be provided with something to do in keeping with his limited capabilities. He must also feel that what he is being asked to do is a useful and meaningful task. He should see the results of his efforts as in some way benefiting himself and others. To clarify this point, let me cite an example: A young man has been quite severely injured as a result of his service to his country in the war effort staged in Vietnam. He has lost a leg, is badly disfigured facially, is mising several fingers and part of his ear. His general appearance is such that others shy away from any contact with him. His mental faculties are sound, but will not remain so if he must face continued rejection in his effort to prove his usefulness. He has tried, unsuccessfully, to work as a clerk in a shoestore. The public who came into contact with him were sufficiently disturbed by his appearance to withdraw their patronage from the store. In order to salvage his business, his employer regrettably terminated the clerk's position. This is a very unfortunate situation for a young man to be faced with; in addition to his physical problems, his mental health is now being challenged. To be rehabilitated, he must be allowed to prove his own self-worth. Sympathy from others will do no good. Unemployment compensation is not a valid answer. The young man needs to know that he can contribute, maintain himself, and be a useful member of society. He is no longer able to function as he did prior to his injuries, but he is still capable of performing some task, however simple, for which he can achieve a measure of success. Fortunately, my story does have a happy ending as the young man in question responded to a request for a disabled veteran to fill the position of mail clerk for a large insurance company. He was hired and daily made his rounds to deliver the mail. It did not take long for the other employees to react to his enthusiastic attitude, brought about as a result of his receiving the position, and they soon stopped noticing his physical defects. The position was not in keeping with his intellectual capabilities, but it was the first step in breaking down barriers that exist because of man's inhumanity to his less fortunate peers.

Whenever possible, one should be allowed to function at the peak of his mental capacity, but where there are physical handicaps, it is best to try to stay within the bounds they present and to deal with the situation on the basis of the disability, as the first order of priority. It is always important to consider an individual's intellectual ability when hiring an employee. To deviate from this, except in situations as just presented, can cause the person hired to become bored and, therefore, uninterested in performing his assigned task. The degree of difficulty of the position should be matched with aptitude test scores of the prospective employee. We all need a challenge in our daily lives to keep us on our toes and in a state of anticipation. Without such an outlet, we become lethargic and displeased with the world around us. If we are satisfied with our lot and living to the fullest, we will not be inclined to resort to complaining or to seeking a means of escape from our daily routine. We will be content to take each day as it comes and to do our best in all of our undertakings. We will wear a smile on our face and be able to ignore those who resort to less desirable manifestations of their situations.

The need to allow for human dignity must never be overlooked. It should be the prime consideration in all of our efforts to overcome the problems of mankind. However, we must start with our own John Doe, private citizen, before we can begin to concern ourselves with the people of other countries. We constantly demand that nations preserve the dignity of their citizens, yet we have fallen short of fulfilling this need on the homefront. We would be wise to put our own house in order and endeavor to set an example that others will want to follow, rather than expecting them to do as we say; not as we do. We still have a long way to go in providing for the retarded, the elderly, and the less fortunate members of the minority groups in our society. We have let poverty run rampant; we have failed to make inroads in the unemployment situation; we offer only token employment to minority groups; we refuse to allow equal rights for women to become a part of our constitution; and still we set ourselves up as a country capable of telling others how to solve their problems. The dignity of our own countrymen must be the first order of business, before we try to undertake any task that extends beyond our territorial boundaries.

The inalienable rights of our citizens have never been truly respected and have, therefore, always been a source of tension. Many have suffered unnecessary hardships in their efforts to exercise their freedom of choice. They have often been denied the right to follow a given profession or to live in an area that best suited their needs. Many have found themselves at the mercy of others, as they strugled to fulfill their personal goals. Yet, no man should be subject to the whims of another, nor should he be subservient to another's demands. Each of us has the right to live as we choose, to work in an occupation that is in keeping with our innate abilities; and to take up residence in any area that we select; without the need to request permission for such action. We must be free to move about without fear of reprisal. The Earth belongs to no man. It is to be shared equally by all of its inhabitants.

"Live and let live" is an axiom that we would all be wise to follow. We must learn to give up our attempts to infringe on the rights of others. We can start in our own house, with our own families, to show respect for each individual and to allow them to live in the manner that best suits their talents and desires. Respect for one's fellow man will bring with it an increased awareness of the dignity of all members of the human race and provide for an ongoing desire to improve the conditions under which we all must live.

Chapter Three
Let Freedom Reign

The right to be free is every man's dream. We do not dwell on this premise as much as the people of other countries for we are blessed with this quality in our lives and we take it pretty much for granted. Still, Americans traveling abroad are always glad to return. The contrast with the way of life that others must endure makes them truly believe that "there is no place like home". Ours is one of the few countries where individual rights are respected. Those of us who never have an opportunity to experience life as it is lived in nations under the domination of government controls do not truly appreciate what we have. We hear a lot about what is happening to oppressed peoples who live in fear of reprisal should they try to stand up for their rights as individuals, yet this does not necessarily make us more thankful for our own rights to life, liberty, and the pursuit of happiness.

There is so much that should be done to insure freedom throughout the world, but we cannot bring about the changes needed by force, coercion, or even promises of essential goods and services. We have tried all of these methods to no avail. Time and time again, we have endeavored to put an end to hostilities between nations. We have entered into peace treaties, peace missions, detente, and arms limitation agreements, but it has all been in vain. Armed conflicts continue all over the globe; somewhere, someone is always at odds with another country. Peace among nations seems to be wishful thinking. As one of the super-powers, we should be setting an example for others to follow, but we have failed in this role by our refusal to refrain from intervention into the affairs of other nations. We have participated in wars that had nothing to do with preserving our territorial rights. We have tried to influence politics in other countries so that those governments would function in accord with our idea of what was best for both their nation and ours. We have used means of reprisal that in no way reflected the rights of men to live in accord with their own philosophical beliefs. We have failed to truly understand other cultures and have tried to force our ideals upon them. We have resorted to murder, assassination, and "dirty tricks" as a means of gaining our own end. We are dishonest in our trade dealings; selling where we claim to boycott because of another country's infringement on personal liberty. What we do and what we say we do tend to be at opposite ends of the spectrum. As we take a stand against hostilities between countries, we supply them with arms and ammunition so that they may carry on their wars. We are not trying to maintain peace when we are the source of supply of the means of continuing the conflict. We do not want others to know of our involvement and deny accusations of assistance, but we do not fool other governments; they are aware of our double standard. No wonder we have lost our credibility with the "powers that be" in the rest of the world. How can we expect other countries to look up to us and respect us as a nation dedicated to the cause of freedom for all mankind? Actually, about all that we can hope to do, once we have set our own affairs in order, is to take steps to enhance the effectiveness of the United Nations or to promote the establishment of a World Council (see Chapter Six) dedicated to the advancement of human rights. However, it will require the cooperation of each individual country in order for them to work out their own salvation.

If we can conquer the obstacles that we face on the home-front, surely the people of other nations can do the same; their battle will be no harder than ours. They have free will, just as we do, and must begin to exercise this God-given right if they are to overcome their plight.

Some of the people whom we feel are being mistreated are quite content with their lot; they do not want things to change. This is something we must take into consideration when we endeavor to become involved in the affairs of others. Freedom has different meanings for different people. For us it is the right to come and go as we please, to own property. to be able to travel to other countries, to attend the place of worship of our choice, to work at the occupation we consider most suitable to our capabilities, to receive a fair wage, and to be able to go to the college or university we deem in keeping with our educational needs. For those in some countries, freedom means not being a slave, not being incarcerated, and not being forced to labor unmercifully or without remuneration. When we think of freedom, we cannot think of it in our terms for all mankind. There are many people who could not cope with our concept of freedom if it were granted to them in one fell swoop. Each nation must start from their individual position to work toward what to them means a step forward in releasing their people from any form of bondage.

We had to work to get where we are, let others have the same opportunity to fight for their rights. The strongest peoples of the world are those who have had to struggle for their freedom. This is not to say that this is an ideal condition, to be inflicted on all men, but it does provide for the survival of the fittest. Strength of character, courage, and dedication of purpose have brought many through times of adversity. These traits will continue to enable men to improve their lot. Those who do not care to take a stand may fall by the wayside, but it will be of their own choosing.

According to Mr. Webster, to be free means: not to be subject to an arbitrary power; not to be a slave or a serf; to enjoy political independence; not to be subject to some particular authority or obligation, hence being released from any onerous conditions. In order to protect our freedom, we, as a nation, must endeavor to become self-sufficient in all areas as soon as possible. It is fine to be able to share in the natural resources of the rest of the world, but until a World Bank (see Chapter One) is established for this purpose, we had better eliminate our dependence on other nations for essential commodities. We will never be truly "free" until this has been accomplished. We may have to do without some of our heretofore taken for granted luxuries, but it will be better than having to do without the basic necessities should we be faced with a curtailment of goods from our present suppliers in other lands. We are all well aware of the dangers we face if we do not cease to allow ourselves to be so vulnerable. We must harken back to the prelude to our Constitution as a way of re-establishing our purpose as a nation:

> *We, the people of the United States, in order for form a more perfect union, establish justice, insure domestic tranquility, provide for the common defense, promote the general welfare, and secure the blessings of liberty to ourselves and our posterity, do ordain and establish this Constitution for the United States of America.*

We will never live up to what our forefathers strived to achieve for our nation if we do not disassociate ourselves from any involvement with other countries and cease to rely on them to provide us with those commodities we deem necessary to our survival.

We have a right to be free; we also have a right not to be free. For example: there are inmates in our prisons who are repeat offenders because they have no desire to be in the outside world; they want to be just where they are. Freedom for them is not something to strive for. These people should in someway be made to earn their keep, as should all others who are incarcerated.

To be free to do as one pleases, without regard for the consequences, is currently an accepted way of life for the young people of our country. It is a no holds barred, no questions asked situation. This attitude prevails throughout our entire public school system where discipline has given way to one's God-given right to such immunity. However, this kind of independence can be detrimental to all concerned for to be free must also carry with it responsibility for one's actions. As an illustration of how we are misusing freedom in our schools, let me tell you of one day in my life as a substitute teacher for a group of teenagers who had been banned from the local high school and sent to an alternative school to complete their studies. They were the "bad kids" who could not conform to the rules and regulations set down by society for acceptable behavior. They were isolated from the majority of their peers and labeled potential high school drop-outs. Still, if they were willing to do a prescribed amount of work, they could eventually earn a high school diploma; a piece of paper that would enable them to be more acceptable in the job market. Most of the students did not want to do very much work; they preferred to play poker, shoot pool, drink coffee, and smoke cigarettes – all of which was accepted as part of the day's routine. A few were conscientious about trying to complete assignments and one wondered why they were in such a situation.

Set apart in an unstructured school, these young adults acted out their individual frustrations and, if nothing else, were kept off the streets and out of trouble for a part of the day. They came and went as they pleased; transportation being the only factor that made for any scheduling. Those who rode the school bus had to adhere to its times for arrival and departure, others stayed for the morning, some came just for the afternoon, and still others attended an evening session once or twice a week. The teachers were very patient, tolerating behavior and language that would be frowned upon in the traditional classroom. Little respect was shown for the teachers, they were addressed by their given name and any requests that they made for a change of behavior were generally ignored. The so-called "students" conversations revolved around last nights party, the amount of alcohol consumed, the availability of drugs, and run-ins with the local law enforcement officers.

What is happening to our society? Why is such permissiveness granted to those who do not care to abide by the established rules for appropriate conduct? What are we accomplishing by spoon-feeding these young offenders? Why should they be given special privileges because they choose to ignore conventional restrictions? They may be the unfortunate victims of a difficult childhood or an unsatisfactory home environment, but what are they going to achieve by this further lack of respect for discipline? Certainly, it is helpful to have them removed from a structured school curriculum where they are a disruptive force to those who are trying to work and to the teacher who is endeavoring to instruct a class. Still, there must be something else that can be done to solve this problem. Granted, these young people may have a poor self-image, but this is not going to be overcome until they have an opportunity to prove their worth by becoming useful and contributing members of their communities. Rather than tolerating their negative behavior, standards should be set for them to meet in order to complete their education; special privileges should be bestowed for merit and goals achieved.

A contractual arrangement could be established whereby each individual who is assigned to the alternative school makes an agreement with the teacher as to what he is willing to do in exchange for certain privileges. It should be a progressive program of increased rewards for continued adherence to an agreed-upon performance. This would give each individual an opportunity to choose his own goals and his own time frame for the completion of the work involved. It would teach him to make choices about his own life as well as give him an opportunity to prove his ability to live up to what he has assented to in a written and signed contract. Failure to abide by said contract would result in the withholding of any rewards.

A contract is a very valuable tool to use in teaching self-discipline. It makes the signer aware of the fact that he is responsible for his own actions and also gives meaning and purpose to his life. A contract can be very simple with an easily achieved termination date. It can then be re-negotiated as is, or revised, for an extended period of time. This enables the individual to reexamine his goals and objectives on a periodic basis, as well as to continually be able to fulfill his obligations. The contract may be written for the number of hours that will be spent on school assignments each day; to designate the number of credits to be earned in a specified time; it may be used as a means to improve personal grooming or behavior; whatever area the student wishes to work on should be acceptable. The reward system should be in line with the commitment made and allow for increased freedom from restrictions and additional recreational privileges as the student improves in his performance.

Life is made up of a series of commitments or contracts and the sooner one learns to live with this concept, the better he will be able to function in society. We make a contract when we enter into marriage, become affiliated with an organization, make any purchase on credit terms, acquire a driver's license, accept a position, enter a school of higher learning, rent a dwelling, start a business, and many, many other facets of our lives are committed to some form of contractual agreements. Why shouldn't our young adults be subject to this same concept in their daily lives; it makes more sense than letting them run rampant with no regard for their own actions and the effect they have on others.

Freedom must be earned, not handed out on a silver platter. Freedom that is misused must be removed. Freedom in the sense that no man must be subservient to another's wishes, is every man's right. Freedom to ignore the laws of the land is no man's right. Freedom carries with it the responsibility of respect for others. "Free to be me" is fine as long as it does not infringe on the rights of one's fellow man. We are free to destroy ourselves, we are not free to destroy another human being. We may choose to inflict damage to our own property, but we may not do the same to that belonging to another person. Our country was founded on the premise that all men should be free, but it was not based on freedom as we know it today. We must return to the true meaning of the Declaration of Independence and put an end to the present disregard for all that is not ours. Freedom will only reign when the evils that beset us are removed for all time. Then freedom will no longer be a threat to our society, but will be a blessing to all who have earned the privilege of living with the true meaning of the word – the right to live in peace with their fellow man and to know the joy of a life devoid of want and need and unnecessary hardships.

Chapter Four
Overcoming The Evils That Plague Our Society

We would all be wise to sit back and take a look at the direction in which we are heading. Is the road we have chosen going to lead us to a happy and contented life or is it one that harbors many pitfalls and eventual disaster? If we feel that we are on the right tract, we can continue on as we are; if not, we should give serious consideration to altering our course. Each of us chooses his own path. We all have free will and, therefore, have the ability to change our ways if we find ourselves in a situation that is not to our liking. All it takes is the determination to do so. Every man is responsible for himself and cannot blame others for the mistakes that he makes. Many have overcome the error of their ways and have gone on to live useful and purposeful lives. They seem to have been granted a second chance at living. Some have sunk to the very depths of despair before making a decision to change. It does not matter at what time in life one decides to seek a better way, what is important is that the change does occur. Those who are unwilling to put an end to their deviant behavior will never know the joy of living with peace and happiness, nor will they command the respect they so ardently desire. They will just sink deeper and deeper into a state of desolation until life has no meaning and all desire for their own salvation is lost forever.

At times, it is very difficult for an individual to face the reality of his negative behavior. He is so certain tht he is right, that those who are not in accord with him are out of step with life and are to be pitied. He will attempt to induce others to try his way, assuring them that it will lead to their enjoying life to the fullest. He will convert some to his lifestyle, others will not be easily influenced and will reject the temptations set before them.

It is not always easy to recognize when we are being led astray. We may have to experience some of the accompanying pitfalls before becoming aware of the mistakes we have made in allowing ourselves to be so easily involved in the wrong kind of a lifestyle. For some, it may take years of living with grief and misery until they are able to break free from the hold that is entombing them. Others will go through life with a minimum of difficulty. They seem to have a built-in sensing unit that keeps them from accepting any negative experiences for themselves. But this does not necessarily make them better people than those who have strayed from the path of decency and then mended their ways. The latter, once they are able to overcome their downhill slide to self-destruction, are usually more tolerant, patient, and compassionate individuals. They seek to help others who are trying to rehabilitate themselves. We have an excellent example of this in the work done by members of Alcoholics Anonymous. These people have experienced the depths of despair and can truly appreciate the meaning of living in a manner that brings them true peace and happiness. What they sought to find in the escape of alcohol they can much better experience by living free from its destructive forces. They are very willing to share their new found knowledge with their fellow man. They now have a purpose in life and no longer have a need to fill their days with useless self-indulgence.

The way we choose to live our lives has a great deal to do with the nature of our personality. Some people are aggressive, enthusiastic, self-starters; while others are shy, inhibited, and lacking in motivation. One is no better than the other. We have a need for both extroverts and introverts in our society. The extroverts will be the leaders; the introverts the followers. We must learn to accept these personality differences and to respect each individual's right to live in accord with his basic character traits. There is no way that we can change others to fit our mold, if they are not of our same makeup. As long as we live in keeping with our innate desire, all will be well. It is only when we try to suppress these needs that a problem arises. The extrovert who attempts to ignore his outward-going nature and finds himself in a confining situation will want to rebel and allow his natural instincts to flow. The introvert, placed in a leadership position, will, no doubt, suffer from feelings of inadequacy. He may resort to a variety of escapist methods in an effort to overcome his own self-doubt. We are what we are. We must learn to accept this fact and be content with our God-given characteristics. Only then will we be able to live in harmony with ourselves and refrain from yielding to any pressures to do that which is not in keeping with our basic nature.

As we make our way in the world, there will be many temptations set before us. At times, it may be difficult to make the right decision in order to avoid those areas that will be detrimental to our well-being. There is a way that we can use to tell if something is going to be to our disadvantage, even though it has all the appearances of being of a harmless nature. First, we should ask ourselves if what we are considering doing will in any way cause us physical harm, feelings of guilt and anxiety, or if it is against our basic philosophical beliefs? What is wrong for one person because of his cultural ways may not be wrong for another. What causes one individual feelings of guilt may in no way affect another's moral code. We all live by different standards, different ethnic values, and we all have a need to be in harmony with our basic personality traits. So, as you contemplate a move that is not in accord with your value system, you must decide if it will cause you any anguish because of your breaking away from your own built-in feelings of right and wrong. It is one thing to grow through new experiences and to change your values and goals in keeping with your increased knowledge and understanding, but that is not the same as plunging blindly into a situation that is foreign to your nature. Therefore, you would be wise to proceed with caution before entering into any grandiose plans that offer silver linings to all life's problems.

There is much evil in our world. It is of the utmost importance that we learn to recognize it and to avoid it at all cost. Not to do so will leave us open to its destructive ways. But, unfortunately, evil is not always recognizable. It is often a source of apparent goodwill and kindness. Evil wears a false facade as it presents itself as our true friend and benefactor. It offers sympathy and comfort in time of need in an effort to entrap us into feeling grateful and subservient for favors rendered. Now this is not to say that no man should trust another. There are many good, kind people who will be only too willing to help us in time of adversity, but they will not seek any recompense for their assistance. They will do what needs to be done to help and then withdraw their services as soon as the emergency is terminated. Evil, on the other hand, will hang on and try to become somewhat of a bloodsucker from which it is very difficult to detach oneself. Evil will continue to make us feel dependent, obligated, and constantly keep us answering to its demands for our time, energy, and possibly even financial contributions to its cause. If it has its own way, evil will not allow a free spirit to remain free. It binds individuals and tries to deprive them of their true identity and purpose in life. It drains one's spirit of its potential for living with joy and happiness and replaces it with servitude and shackles. Evil destroys a man's soul. It can kill in devious ways that are not obvious to others. When an individual becomes mentally ill, severely depressed, or in a state of acute anxiety, he could very well be under the influence of an evil person. This same person may offer a great deal of concern and affect a manner of compassionate understanding, but beware of such false pretensions of human kindness. An evil person does not want to bring about a cure for the disturbed individual; he is more apt to want to bring about his demise without anyone being able to point a finger at him as being the culprit. It would be nice to live in a world free from evil and temptation, but before we can achieve this ideal state, we must learn to avoid such influences and prevent them from entering our lives. Only then will the power of evil be diminished. Bloodsuckers cannot survive without a victim. Temptation, with no one to tempt, would soon lose its impact. So beware of allowing these forces to take hold of your life. Do not succumb to any unnatural or over-solicitous behavior. It is best to stay within your own cultural community and to live with your own philosophical beliefs as a guide to determining your realm of acceptable experience.

Much of the evil that is rampant in today's society has been allowed to flourish because of our disregard for our fellow man and our reluctance to take a stand on issues that are undermining the basic human values by which previous generations chose to live. We do all this in the name of individual rights and feel no need to assume any responsibility for what is happening. We are aghast at the reports of violent behavior that daily flood our news media, but equally as destructive is the immoral behavior with which we are faced. We seem to think that we can disregard all forms of common decency. However, what we neglect to consider is the overall decline of morals as a source of national deterioration.

Free sex became rampant as a way of life in the 1960's. It was not a new innovation. This same type of behavior was in vogue at the time of the decline of the Roman Empire. A high degree of sexual freedom was the prerogative of both men and women of that era. Marriage and divorce were easily manipulated. When Nero, the ruler of Rome from 54 to 68 A.D., expressed his opinion that chastity and purity did not exist, he was describing the upper class society of his time. Therefore, it is not surprising to note that while Nero fiddled and Rome burned in the Big Fire of 64 A.D., all the court was engaged in an ongoing orgy of sex and wine. We are fast following in the footsteps of ancient Rome. Let us hope that we do not meet with the same disastrous end.

Today we place little value on the true meaning of a loving relationship between a man and a woman. The stability of the family as a unit is declining. Children are often the by-product of casual sex, not wanted by either parent. Abortion is becoming the accepted way of dealing with the problem. No doubt it is better than bringing an unwanted child into today's world, but it would be far better if such a decision were not necessary; except in the case of a medical prognosis of possible death or injury to the mother, or a malformed fetus that would not have a chance of a normal existence. Another negative result of free sex is the escalation of sex related diseases. Unfortunately, this can have lasting ill effects on its victim. True, there are drugs that can be used to overcome some of these incidents, but not all respond to such treatment. Too often, it is a case of the punishment being much greater than the pleasure derived from the act itself. To be a meaningful experience, sex should be a way to enhance a commitment between a man and a woman who are willing to establish a relationship that will have lasting ties.

Sex, alcohol, and drugs seem to be foremost in the minds of a vast majority of our young people. The thrill of partaking of those things that have been labeled "forbidden fruit" is their way of finding an outlet for their growing frustration with the condition of our society. They have very little to look forward to and thus have little purpose or motivation to seek out future goals. Most of them have serious doubts about the very survival of our planet and they have justifiable reason for this concern. Home, family, church, and school are meaningless to most of the younger generation. Why bother with these outmoded barriers to their individual rights to do as they please, when they please, and with whom they please? To live for today is their only desire. They have become a generation of pleasure seekers. They have succumbed to the temptations that offer them the means of escape from reality, responsibility, and the very reason for their being. It is truly a sad and frightening situation. These are the future leaders of our country and we have allowed them to become so disenchanted with their prospective role that one wonders if there is any hope for their salvation.

Somehow we must put an end to all of this waste of human potential. We must create an atmosphere of loving concern for the well-being of our young people and make them realize their value as human beings, as well as their obligation to the human race. This will not be an easy task, but it will be well worth all of the effort that it takes. It does no good to preach, cajole, punish, or to extole the virtues of an alternate lifestyle. What is needed is a goal, a purpose, a feeling of being an important part of the preservation of our environment and natural resources. We must call upon the youth of this country, not to serve in the armed forces, but to serve for the betterment of conditions with which we all must live.

We cannot delay in our efforts to bring about a plan of action that will involve today's youth in tomorrow's cause. Instead of drafting potential soldiers for the armed services, we would be wise to create a volunteer force, similar to the Peace Corps, whose services would be utilized within the territorial boundaries of the fifty states. The Peace Corps had its inception on October 14, 1960. Those who practice astrology will note that it was conceived under the sign of Libra, which is characterized by a passion for fairness, refusal to compromise on principles, special genius in the field of human relations, and a gentle courtesy. It was at this time that John F. Kennedy, then a presidential candidate, addressed a group of students at Ann Arbor, Michigan. He spoke about the need for a better understanding between nations and of his belief that America should take the lead in befriending the underdeveloped countries of the world. "I would like America to form a Peace Corps of volunteers – young people with ideals and enthusiasm – who will give two years of their lives to humanity." He then asked how many of the students would be willing to help to accomplish such a plan. The cheers and applause that followed left no doubt as to their enthusiastic acceptance of this challenge.

On November 2, 1960, during a major speech at the Cow Palace in San Francisco, Kennedy announced that one of the first major acts as president would be to establish an organization of American volunteers for overseas service; for peaceful purposes. Campaign promises are often forgotten by the people who make them; this one was not. Thousands of letters and telegrams poured into Washington from young individuals who wanted to volunteer. On September 22, 1961, also under the sign of Libra, the Peace Corps Act was passed and Congress appropriated $30,000,000 to fund the new organization for the first year.

During the summer of 1961, the first 300 volunteers were selected. Some people called these young recruits idealists. And so they were. They believed that the underprivileged people of all races, creeds, and cultures deserved assistance in creating a better life for themselves. They were ready to teach, to be health workers, to build bridges, and to perform any other necessary tasks. Their goal was to wipe out hunger, disease, and ignorance; those things that threaten peace. The broad concept of the Peace Corps is that unequal standards of living among nations is a very real cause of war. Thus, by helping nations to improve their circumstances, the cause of peace is fulfilled.

It was decided that the Peace Corps volunteers would only go where they were invited. And countries asked for them. New countries, underdeveloped countries, and those who needed help in train- their own people. Soon trained volunteers were moving out to remote areas to begin the difficult, but rewarding, adventure of living and working with people of other lands. They helped them to acquire new skills, to develop changed attitudes, to achieve a sense of personal dignity, and to set their own goals.

The purpose of the Peace Corps, as defined by law, is:

1. To help the people of interested countries meet their need for trained manpower.

2. To help promote a better understanding of the American people on the part of the people being served.

3. To promote a better understanding of other people on the part of the American people.

In 1960, the Peace Corps was only an idea. Today it is a people-helping-people program that has brought skills to the unskilled; friendship to the friendless; and hope to the hopeless.

A similar organization to work within the confines of the United States, with the goal of protecting our environment, our natural resources, and our human dignity, would, no doubt, meet with much enthusiasm. Upon completion of their education, young men and women would have an opportunity to voluntarily enlist for two years in an unarmed army with financial remuneration and benefits equal to those offered by our existing regular armed services. Very few would turn down such an assignment. However, it is to be hoped that some would find other useful endeavors to pursue, as there will always be a need for their services in the mainstream of society.

Once we have provided an outlet for the energies of our up and coming generation, we will begin to see a change in their attitudes and behavior. Some may choose to remain in the "new army" after their tour of duty has ended. They can then move up in their area of interest and assume positions of responsibility in recruiting, training, and placing of new volunteers. Others will emerge as leaders. There are always those who rise up within a group and take the initiative in whatever project is involved. And so, we will not only be providing motivation to our young people to be of service, we will also be establishing a training ground for the future leaders of our communities, states, and country.

It is never too soon to begin to make amends for wrongs that have been done. We must start now to take some action that will help to overcome the evil that exists within our sphere of influence. We knew what measures were necessary to stamp out the plague when the first epidemic in the United States struck San Francisco's Chinatown in 1900; and no man hesitated to take them. Why then should we be hesitant about doing all in our power to overcome the even more insidious plague that is undermining our very planet? As soon as the epidemic was reported, a cordon was established around Chinatown and the area was cleaned as never before. Every house in the district was scrubbed from the rooftop to the basement with a very strong chemical and was then sprayed with mercuric chloride. All household goods were removed and aired for several days or were sterilized by steam and disinfectant. Dark rooms and cellars were whitewashed. The residences of the plague victims were fumigated with sulphur dioxide for forty-eight hours. In all, twelve thousand houses and fourteen thousand rooms were treated. By 1904, the epidemic had been wiped out; no new cases were reported and, once again, life in Chinatown was back to normal.

A united effort succeeded in bringing about an end to the plague in San Francisco and it will take the same kind of a united effort to bring about the elimination of evil in our society. We must all band together in a crusade to wipe out those areas that are a threat to our continued existence. Each of us has an obligation to participate in such an endeavor. It is the only way that we can overcome the evil that besets us.

Chapter Five
"To Be Or Not To Be"

"To be or not to be, that is the question" is a famous Shakespearean quotation that has been passed down through the ages and exemplifies the dilemma with which we are confronted in all areas of our lives. Should we become involved or should we remain silent and passively carry on our own affairs while the world around us becomes more and more chaotic? Why become implicated? What good will it do? No one individual can make a contribution that will in any way aid the cause of all mankind. It is enough of an undertaking to try to sustain ourselves. Let others worry about their own survival. As long as we are in no way threatened, why not just stay quietly uninvolved? This is not a negative attitude. We, in essence, are only responsible for ourselves and those of our immediate family. If we can manage to live peacefully in our own environment, we are doing all that is required of us as individuals. Not everyone feels challenged to save the world. Those who choose not to become involved are exercising their right of free choice. Those who decide to risk the challenge that involvement is bound to create do so voluntarily and should not expect to receive a great deal of gratitude for their efforts.

It should be accepted as an individual's right to choose when, where, and how he will lend assistance to another person who does not fall under his realm of responsibility. Anyone electing to give service to others should do so with an attitude of quiet concern and a desire to help those who are less fortunate. One should give willingly without any thought of increased self-esteem or appreciation for the job undertaken. Such rewards are not to be considered the reason for aiding one's fellow man. Those who do have a personal motive for their supposed good deeds are not to be admired or emulated, as they only help individuals who are in a position to bring them prestige. They become so impressed with their benevolent works that they expect others to follow in their footsteps and belittle those who choose not to do so. Anyone receiving the benefit of your assistance should in no way be obligated to you for more than their sincere appreciation and thanks at the time of being the recipient of your good will. They must not feel beholden to you on an ongoing basis for what you have voluntarily chosen to contribute to improve their well-being. There is no need to "blow your own horn" and boast of the magnitude of your generosity. If self-satisfaction is your only motive, then you may as well forsake any good deeds as they are not being done in a true spirit of love and concern. The only reward you should expect to receive is the personal satisfaction of helping a less fortunate person in his hour of need.

There are times when some of us become so enmeshed in the problems of other individuals that we forget that we are not totally responsible for their welfare. We lose sight of our own reason for being. We must provide for and protect our children until they are able to care for themselves, but this is the only time that we should be completely in control of another person's life; and it is only for a limited period. Once our children have reached the age of eighteen, we must free them from our parental supervision and allow them to pursue their own way in the world. Whether or not their goals are to our liking should not be our prime concern; their ability to maintain themselves is what is important.

We all want to be free to follow whatever course of action our innate desire challenges us to accept and to live in the manner in which we feel most content. We, in turn, must allow others to pursue their choice of personal goals. We must not try to force our aims or lifestyle on another person. What works for one individual may not prove to be in the best interest of another. Man is a very complex species, no two are the same. Even identical twins have their different personality traits. We should learn to accept each individual's uniqueness and forget about trying to change or mold people into our own image. Unless they are in some way harming themselves or others, we should refrain from trying to alter the habits of another person. To do so can be the cause of much dissatisfaction in the lives of those whom we find ourselves in a position to dominate, either by our financial assistance or the guilt feelings we impose on a family member or friend who does not do our bidding. No man should be subservient to another.

A person who is self-destructive or a menace to society must be answerable to the community in which he resides and proper medical or penal action should be taken to keep him from his pernicious ways. This action should never be considered to be the responsibility of his family or friends. We are not our brother's keeper in the sense that we are to be a police person who will protect him from himself.

Life is to be enjoyed; human sacrifice is not a noble trait. Do not let others prevail upon your good nature and take advantage of your inability to say "no" to their every demand made upon you. It takes a strong individual to stand up for his right to remain independent and free from feelings of guilt for not acquiescing to every request made for his time, talent, or financial contribution. This is not to say that you should refuse assistance of an immediate nature, but to go beyond the essential requirements for "first aid" is not anyone's responsibility. To do so may seem like an act of kindness, still it may not be in the best interest of the person involved. It is fine to help others and to provide them with food and shelter for a limited period of time; more than that may deprive them of their need to be accountable for themselves. It takes away from an individual's self-respect to have another person provide for all of his wants and can bring about feelings of resentment, rather than appreciation.

We are responsible for our own well-being. We cannot expect others to do for us what we can do for ourselves; nor should we attempt to do for others what they can do for themselves. Mental cripples have been made of normal, healthy individuals by over-protecting them from the adversities of life. To never allow a person to suffer the consequences of his own actions is to forever bind him to the hand that defends him. We all learn from our mistakes if we are allowed to suffer the ill effects. Hopefully we will refrain from making the same error all over again. Many of the misfits in our society today are the result of over-protection. They have never learned to stand on their own two feet and to accept their fate as it is unfurled. They always place the blame for their failings on someone else and never consider themselves liable for any misfortune that comes their way. The more such behavior is reinforced, the more it becomes a fixed pattern that is virtually impossible to break. The person playing the protective role may tire of the noose around his neck but he will have very little chance of escaping his self-induced slavery. Often this type of individual thrives on such a demanding presence in his life, the need to be needed is his ego's way of maintaining its superior status. "If it were not for me," is the name of the game. Such a person is as much of a menace to society as is his victim.

There is a very fine line between what is and what is not in the realm of one's responsibility. There are times when it is wise to take a stand and make yourself heard on a particular issue. There are times when it is in the best interest of all concerned to lend a helping hand. The best way to determine the advisability of your becoming involved is to ask yourself if what you are planning to do will benefit others or will it be solely for your own need to be self-serving to your ego?

"Fools rush in where angels fear to tread" is an old adage that we would all be wise to heed; "look before you leap" is another. We are often too quick to give advice or try to take charge of a situation in which we have no reason to be involved. Unsolicited advice is never worth its salt; actually, it may cause more harm than good. Should you feel the need to speak out on an issue that involves you, that is your privilege. However, if it is not of your individual concern, you would be wise to hold your tongue unless your advice is requested. The person who asks your opinion is under no obligation to do as you suggest; he may want to consider a variety of options before reaching a decision. We always think that we know what is best for others to do, but it is a rare occasion when we can give the right solution to their dilemma. We should not risk the possibility of being held responsible for causing unnecessary problems by giving the wrong advice. It is best to preface your ideas with "you might want to consider", or, "have you given any thought to", as a way of not being too forceful in your opinions. If your suggested solution is then acted upon, it will be done because it seemed to be the right course to follow, and not because you insisted that it be done in such a manner. If it does not work out satisfactorily, you will not be to blame. We may want to be helpful; our intentions may be of the best; but, nevertheless, that does not make us infallible. We cannot foresee the outcome of what we are advocating. We might think we know what will happen in a given situation, but nothing is fixed and there are always extenuating circumstances that can alter seemingly obvious answers.

Just as we must tread lightly in giving of our advice, so must we avoid falling into the trap of letting others tell us what to do and what not to do. No one truly knows what is right for another person. The sooner we learn to stand up for our rights in all areas of our lives, the happier we will be.

We often look upon the care of the elderly as the responsibility of their offspring. Some older people are able to acclimate themselves to the lifestyle of the younger generation and cause little or no change in the existing household. They are welcome and contributing members of the family. Others, by the very nature of their personalities, act as a destructive force that cannot be reckoned with and their behavior does not lend itself to maintaining a harmonious household. They refuse to give up the role of the dominating parent and expect to be catered to until their dying day. The more they are able to succeed, the more demanding they become. If allowed to continue with their antics, they often disrupt the domestic scene and cause marital problems. They rarely appreciate what is done for them and enjoy their own chronic complaining. Such negative persons should either maintain their own homes, live in a senior citizen complex, or take up residence in a nursing home if this type of care is required. Families should suffer no feelings of regret or guilt at finding suitable housing for them in other areas. Since nothing is going to make them happy, why bother to play the martyr.

The best way to deal with chronic complainers is to ignore their behavior. If they are unable to arouse sympathy, they will be more apt to give up in their efforts to do so. To feed the fire will only add to their satisfaction in bemoaning their fate.

Society has made provision for the care of the disabled and the infirmed, who cannot afford private assistance, in facilities that are funded by local, state, and federal monies. Whenever possible, families with an individual who falls into these categories would be wise to take advantage of the services available to meet his needs. The indigent person will be just as well cared for as he would be at home without entailing a great deal of self-sacrifice on the part of family members. The people who devote their lives to the care of others, who have chosen this as their life's work, are the ones who should have the responsibility for those who are not able to maintain themselves. It is their gift to their fellow man and should be accepted and appreciated.

We are never content when we are forced to do things that are not in keeping with our inner feelings of what is in our own best interest. To understand our need to live in accord with our own basic nature should help us to realize this same need in all people. We should endeavor to come to terms with the different ideals and beliefs of the individual members of our families as a way to start to have an idea of the differences in all mankind. We might study other cultures, become acquainted with people of various ethnic backgrounds, and welcome them into our homes for an exchange of ideas. When we realize that they have the same basic wants, needs, and goals as we have, we will have a better understanding of why we should not try to prevent them from following their own native customs. We can also visit churches of various denominations, as well as a synagogue, in order to become familiar with individual religious preferences. It will be the beginning of a building up of our tolerance and respect for others. It does not mean that we are to adopt their ways, or they ours, but will serve to develop a realization of the rights of all men to live in accord with their beliefs. Once we have achieved this understanding, we will have a built-in guide to help us to limit our interference in the lives of others. We will know when to step in to offer assistance; we will also know when to forego giving our advice.

The inhabitants of every country should be allowed to live in the manner that best suits their climate, terrain, and philosophical beliefs – whether they be religious or political. What is right for one area is not necessarily right for another. We may consider our lifestyle to be superior and be convinced that it is so ideal that the rest of the world would benefit from following in our footsteps. But this is not so! Individual and ethnic differences must be taken into consideration. To try to change others by forceful means is of no value. We do not want a foreign government to tell us that we must follow their directions; we would surely rebel against such action. Why, then, do we feel that we have a right to impose our will on other nations and expect them to acquiesce to our demands? Granted there is room for improvement in other countries, but there is also room for improvement in our own country. We try to tell other nations how to run their affairs while we are still unable to solve our own problems. It is quite obvious that we do not have all of the answers. We think of ourselves as a super-power, able to influence the rest of the world, but this is a far cry from the truth. We must first practice what we preach and prove the value of our assumptions, before we can expect others to look to us for guidance and to respect the advice we have to offer. When they see that we are meeting with success on the homefront, they may be willing to listen to us. It is our constant desire to reform or remake others that causes so much disharmony.

Because of our technological advances, communication has been developed to such an extent that we are informed of world events within minutes of their happening. Hardly a day goes by without some startling occurrence being reported. Our world has become so small that we are cognizant of situations that our forefathers had no knowledge of and, therefore, caused them no concern. We are not expected to be able to cope with all of the problems that beset the world and, thus, do not have answers or solutions to these crisis situations. We have almost become numb to the trials and tribulations of others and are only concerned with events that affect us personally. We have learned to shut our eyes to that which we cannot control. It is not up to us to save the people of other countries. In time of natural disaster, we may lend assistance to aid in their rehabilitation, but this is only in response to an immediate emergency. We have organizations within our country that are equipped to deal with such situations and we can, if we choose, offer our support to their efforts. However, it is not an obligation that should cause us any feelings of guilt if we choose to remain uninvolved. Our instant knowledge of these happenings does not make us any more responsible for dealing with them than were our ancestors who waited months for the latest news.

Ignorance is bliss. Unfortunately, we are no longer ignorant or blissful and the Earth is not a better place because of this change. Now that we are exposed to all of the news events of the world, we are in a better position to understand the plight of man, but we are no more able to alter the state of things than those who remained shielded from such knowledge. You might try giving up your radio, television, and newspaper for a period of a week or two and just live within the confines of your own immediate environment. It would give you an idea of how people lived prior to the invention of these great contributions to our civilization. You will, no doubt, enjoy the peace of mind that comes from not "knowing", of being concerned with only your own individual needs, and with total un-involvement in the problems that beset the rest of the world.

The wheels of progress have proven to be more devastating to our sensibilities than was ever meant to be. We have come to the end of the line in our quest to "know all", "see all", and "hear all". We cannot put an end to what we have accomplished, but we can terminate our involvement in areas that are not in our realm of responsibility. We will have to turn a deaf ear to the hue and cry of countries who bring their problems to our doorstep. They seek our aid, but do not offer anything in return. It may be "better to give than to receive", but it is not to our advantage to over-extend ourselves at the expense of the welfare of our own people. We would be better off if we were to adopt a policy of isolation in our dealings with other nations. We have no reason to be involved in their affairs; we only need to be concerned with our own well-being.

Chapter Six
The Need For Law And Order

Disregard for law and order has become an accepted way of life in today's society. Crime is on the increase and there seems to be little that we can do to protect ourselves from some form of attack on either our person or our possessions. This lack of respect for the rules established by those in authority is not limited to any one area. It is a part of the local, national, and international scene and steps must be taken, at all levels, to guarantee the safety of every individual. There are ways to overcome the aggressive actions of those who fail to abide by the code of behavior set down as the standard for all to follow. Laws must be enacted and then enforced without any leniency for "special people", or for any country that attempts to use its power as a threat to others.

In our own country, disrespect for the law has reached a point where there is almost a complete lack of desire on the part of offenders to mend their ways. Crime has become rampant and we are unable to deal with the problem by means of our present law enforcement policies. The existing system of "so-called" justice fails to make all criminals equally responsible for their actions. Those of prominence, or. wealth, are more apt to be treated with leniency; some of our penal institutions are run like a rich man's country club. Still, a criminal is a criminal without regard to race, creed, or color, and in all instances should be treated as such. Punishment for a particular crime should be the same for anyone who commits the offense and it should be implemented in the same manner for all offenders. Those members of society who flaunt the laws established for the benefit of all should be isolated from the mainstream of life. They should not be coddled and catered to, but made to realize that they have been incarcerated because of their deviant behavior. Only then will all men realize that they are responsible for their own actions.

We must amend our laws so that once a criminal is found

guilty as charged, he will be sentenced immediately, without any right to bail, should imprisonment be deemed necessary. This may sound harsh and, at times, an injustice may be done, but it will never be as great as the injustice that is caused by allowing those of evil intent to roam the streets once their disregard for the law has been determined. Many drug pushers, rapists, and murderers are free on bail, to continue in their destructive ways, because we have allowed them to be released pending an appeal of the decision made in their case. Until these offenders are dealt with without delay and sentenced according to the predetermined punishment for their offense, we will continue to see our crime rate increase.

One of the greatest causes for concern in our country today is the impact of drugs on the lives of the younger generation; they are so vulnerable to new and forbidden experiences. They ignore all warnings to refrain from "playing with fire" and consider themselves daring and "cool" when they give into peer pressures to try a "joint", or to swallow a pill of questionable potency. If only we could protect them from these destructive experiences, yet we cannot lock our children in the closet or "wrap them in cellophane" to prevent them from being exposed to such influences. What we can do is to mandate our law enforcement officers to take action against drug dealers in a more effective and immediate manner. Once these criminals realize that we mean what we say about removing them from society, they may begin to consider mending their ways. Those who are incarcerated without the possibility of bail, or parole, will be the best deterrent to others to cease their illegal activities.

We know that drugs are "Big Business" in our country and that it is very difficult to locate the source of supply in all instances. However, if we can eliminate the pusher on the street, we will be taking a major step toward reducing the potential harm to our children. Distribution of drugs at this level is the final step in the whole process and is the only one that we, as parents, can hope to be able to control. We must, therefore, take a stand and demand that legal proceedings be enacted to remove these middlemen. It is our right to do so. The days of protecting such offenders must be replaced by an era of severe reprisal. It is the only hope we have of overcoming this crime against our young people.

The increase in crime in today's society has been brought about by the widespread use of drugs. The fact that certain substances are illegal have made their acquisition a prime source of revenue for those involved in organized crime. Consequently, it might be advisable for us to lift the ban on the possession of these drugs and then to prohibit their sale to minors, as we do with alcohol and tobacco. This would not curtail the use of drugs, but it would at least do away with the excess profit that is now being realized by those who are in the business of dealing in these commodities. If the price to the consumer were not so exorbitant, it would eliminate the need for the user to resort to stealing, mugging, and killing in order to meet his need for a "fix". Should he be intent on destroying himself, let him do so without causing harm to others. We had an experience with prohibition that should stand us in good stead in our efforts to control the use of drugs. Just as prohibitive measures did not stop the consumption of alcohol in the 1920's, they will not stop the usage of drugs in the 1980's.

Billions of dollars in profit is being realized each year by those who are in the business of illegal drug trafficking. And it is tax free! Take, for example, a haul of marijuana that did not reach the streets, but was confiscated by customs officials off the coast of Savannah, Georgia. The eighteen tons of "manicured" Columbian "grass", with a street value of forty-five dollars or more an ounce, would have brought in a total of 3.25 million, tax free dollars. Dealing in cocaine can be even more lucrative. Street "coke" of a six to eight percent purity sells for ninety to one hundred twenty-five dollars a gram; thus a two hundred and fifty pound haul of cocaine would net eighty million, tax free dollars. The whole set-up has reached a point that could be termed a national insanity. If we were to legalize the sale of drugs and tax the user for his purchase, the revenue realized by the state and federal governments could be allocated for constructive purposes; such as improving the lot of our indigenous population, or restoring the environment. Whatever use might be decided upon would certainly be better than filling the till of organized crime.

Once the need to supply the demand for drugs by illegal means is removed, they will lose their value as a money-making venture. A whole network of sub-culture activities will be laid to rest. It will, no doubt, rise up in other areas but not to the extent that it has taken hold in drug trafficking. There are those who will argue that by condoning the use of drugs we will be adding to the already obvious decline of our society. How can it become any worse? If it is no longer necessary to steal, to resort to violence, and in some instances, to murder in order to purchase the much-needed fix, we will at least see a drop in the crime rate. This, in itself, will be a saving for the taxpayers who must bear the cost of subsidizing our law enforcement officers, judicial system, and penal institutions. As the use of drugs loses its mystique, intrigue, daring, and status, it will also begin to lose its appeal. It all goes back to that which is forbidden is most desired. We will still have problems, just as we still have problems with alcohol, but they will not be so totally devastating to such a large majority of our population.

No society can exist without the enforcement of its laws. In our own homes we establish rules that enable us to live harmoniously. We also devise some sort of reprimand for family members who refuse to abide by the day-to-day routine standards set for behavior within the household. It is the only way that people who share the same space can live in peace. To destroy each others personal possessions, or to resort to physical violence as a means of settling disagreements would certainly not be in the best interest of the parties involved. On a broader scale, if your neighbor should decide to set fire to your house, it would not be advisable to retaliate by setting fire to his house; nor would it be wise to sit back and not take any action to protest such an infringement on your rights. It would, however, be to your advantage to have the guilty party removed from society until such time as he made amends for the damage he caused. So it should be if one country invades the territorial rights of another. They should not be allowed to resort to such tactics without being censored and dealt with in a manner befitting their infraction of International Law.

International laws are as necessary as local and national laws and must be enforced and adhered to if we are ever to have worldwide peace. Attempts to encroach on the geographical terrain of another country should be swiftly dealt with by a World Council that has the power to administer reprisals for such action. The country responsible for this kind of an offensive attack should be fined in accordance with the degree of its violation; the fine imposed being levied against its account in the World Bank (see Chapter One) that controls the distribution of natural resources. No country is going to be eager to execute an act of aggression if it will mean the curtailment of the delivery of those commodities necessary to its survival. In addition to the penalty imposed, the citizens of the country involved in the altercation should be called upon to cease their aggression and to hold a general election to remove those in positions of authority who are responsible for the existing infraction of international law; to have them incarcerated for as long as is deemed an effective punishment for the crime involved. Failure to do so should result in the continued curtailment of the delivery of commodities needed for the ongoing well-being of all of their countrymen. These actions must be accomplished by peaceful means and supervision for carrying them out should be made available by the World Council if their services are deemed necessary. It would be similar to calling out the National Guard in our own country when a crisis situation exists that must not be allowed to run rampant. An international reserve of well-trained men, representing all countries, should be available for such an emergency situation. They would have the power to incarcerate offenders and to deal with any violence by taking appropriate measures such as: cutting off all supplies;

using roadblocks to deter transportation; infiltrating the area held by the opposing force in order to destroy communication systems and, in general, to disrupt all of their attempts at sabotage. Tear gas would be the most effective means of dealing with any aggressive action against this reserve force. Law and order would, no doubt, be restored within a short period of time and the need for continued intervention would cease.

There will be time when countries will have a legitimate disagreement. If they are unable to work out an amiable solution on their own, a neutral mediator should be appointed by the World Council to assist them in reaching a reconciliation. Everything possible should be done to remove all obstacles to a peaceful solution, based on the principle of maintaining human dignity and individual rights. Failure of the parties involved to reach an agreement would result in the dispute being turned over to the World Council for consideration. A body of twelve men, elected by the Council members to act as judges in such matters, would be asked to render a decision. Refusal to act in accordance with their findings would result in a fine being imposed in the form of a penalty on withdrawals from the World Bank of a specified commodity for a time determined to be in keeping with the offending country's unwillingness to cooperate.

The need for a World Council to maintain law and order on an international level is as vital as is our need for a local police force. If individuals are not capable of policing their own actions, how can we expect countries to act responsibly if they are not subject to penalties for failure to abide by the laws as stated. There will always be those who will try to circumvent the law, however, if the "punishment fits the crime" and is administered to all offenders on an equal basis, we should, in time, see a lessening of man's inhumanity to his fellow man. The United Nations has been active in trying to resolve international problems and in some areas has met with success. However, since they have no means of enforcing any action, they fall short of being a viable tool for international peace. It is the same with their efforts to establish international laws. They have defined many problem areas and devised many worthwhile solutions, but no nation is obliged to use their services, or to abide by their decisions on other than a voluntary basis.

The International Court of Justice is the principal judicial organ of the United Nations. It consists of fifteen judges elected by the General Assembly and the Security Council and sits at The Hague, Netherlands. The peaceful settlement of disputes in conformity with principles of justice and international law is the purpose of the court. Recourse to international justice, however, is optional. If a country does not wish to take part in the proceedings before the court, it does not have to do so. The court has assisted countries in solving a number of legal disputes, but could do much more if the nations were more willing to bring their disputes before it for action.

In 1947, the General Assembly of the United Nations established the International Law Commission for the purpose of progressive development of international law. Originally the Commission had fifteen members, but the number has increased and it is now comprised of twenty-five members who are experts on international law. One of the first topics to be dealt with by the Commission at its first session in 1949 was the high seas and the territorial seas. Work in this area continued until 1956 and came to include the Continental Shelf, the Contiguous Zone, and the conservation of the resources of the sea. A final draft on the Law of the Sea was presented to the eleventh session of the Assembly in 1957. At that time, it was decided to convene a Conference on the Law of the Sea. In view of the wide scope of its work, the Conference established five main conventions to deal with the topics of: innocent passage of ships through territorial waters; the conditions under which freedom of the high seas may be exercised; fishing and conservation of living resources of the high seas; regulating the exploitation and exploration of resources, e.g., offshore oil or pearl-bearing oysters; and settling disputes that may arise regarding these conventions. The final act of the Conference was signed on April 29, 1958. All the Conventions remained open for signing until October 31, 1958. Each Convention was to enter into force thirty days after twenty-two ratifications or assentions were received. However, by the end of 1962, only the Conventions dealing with the conditions under which freedom of the high seas may be exercised and the methods to be used in settling disputes had been put into effect.

It is unfortunate that most of the work that has gone into developing international laws, the rules for their implementation, and a universally accepted code of behavior has not met with a great deal of success. This is not to say that the groundwork that has been laid cannot be acted upon and utilized; much has already been done to ease the way for us to establish international laws and peaceful solutions of international problems that will benefit all mankind. We must have regulations for air and sea travel, for the disposal of waste products and sewage, for the conservation of natural resources, and the preservation of wildlife. International policing will be necessary to see that these rules are adhered to if we are all to share equally in the bounty of the earth. Disregard for these laws will only lead to human suffering and the elimination of man's ability to live in an atmosphere of peaceful co-existence with his fellow man.

What contitutes a crime varies from time to time and from

country to country. Different cultures have varying interpretations of the meaning of an infringement on individual rights. We must learn to respect these differences and to abide by the laws as set down; whether or not we are in accord with them, or question their validity is not a matter of concern to those who have written the standards for the behavior of their countrymen. When we visit another country, we must conduct ourselves in keeping with the laws of its land.

From the beginning of time, man has had his laws; as long as they were adhered to, he lived in relative peace. It was only when he tried to circumvent the rules that he ran into trouble, for then he was duly punished for any infraction. Let us take, as an example, the earliest inhabitants of the islands of Japan. They supposedly came down from the heavens in a boat and are known as the Ainu. It is thought that at one time they inhabited all of Japan; today less than twenty thousand of them remain and they are mostly on the island of Yezo which is north of Honshu, the main island of the Empire. These still primitive people adhere to all of their ancient tribal customs and from them we can derive a great deal of insight into the laws of man in his early stage of development. Blood feuds are not a part of the lifestyle of the Ainu, as individuals usually settle their own disputes. Should an offense of a serious nature be committed, a public trial is held at the home of the chief. The matter is discussed for several days before the chief, with advice from his elders, pronounces judgment and decides the penalty. A death sentence is never inflicted, as death is not considered to be a punishment; pain and disgrace are the usual form of discipline. Trial by ordeal is sometimes used to determine an individuals guilt. The accused person may be required to put his arm into a kettle of boiling water, or to hold a hot stone in his hand; if he is not burned, he is innocent. He may be ordered to drink a cup of water and to throw the empty cup over his shoulder. If it lands right side up, he is innocent; if not, he is guilty. A criminal will, at times, commit suicide rather than face an ordeal. In the case of stealing, the culprit must return the value of the stolen goods and receive a flogging. Should he repeat the offense, he will be ostracized from the community and have the tip of his nose cut off. A murderer may be crippled for life by having the tendons of his feet cut, or he may have his nose or ear removed. It is not hard to understand why serious crimes are almost non-existent among the Ainu.

Perhaps we should not have become so lenient in our system of justice, but it is never to late to mend our ways and to advocate laws in which the punishment will be in keeping with the offense committed. Whether it be in our own backyard, our neighbors backyards, or on the high seas, there is only one way to preserve law and order and that is with complete responsibility being given to the law enforcement agencies to perform their task knowing that they will have the full support of those whom they represent.

Chapter Seven
Nuclear Holocaust

Our world today is in a sad state. Man has come so far in his technological pursuits that he now has the ability to destroy the entire planet with the mere touch of a button. As a result, we all live in fear of just such an incident occurring. Even though we strive to keep our relationships with other nations on an even keel, we do not have any guarantee that we will ultimately be spared the devastation of a nuclear attack. From time to time, we hear of a potentially catastrophic nuclear accident that has been averted, but the fear of an actual incident, being caused by human error, is always with us. There is no doubt that we are on the brink of destroying the whole human race. There seems to be little that we, as individuals, can do to prevent this impending disaster.

Since the beginning of time, man has fought to maintain himself, his family, and his territorial boundaries. His existence on this planet has never really been easy, still it has never been as precarious as it is at present. Wars have always been waged, although they were limited in their scope. Human lives were lost, property was destroyed, great havoc was wrought; nevertheless, life reverted back to its normal state at the cessation of hostilities. A nuclear war today would not find life continuing on this planet. Any who did survive would eventually be overcome by the radioactive fallout that would also destroy all forms of life-sustaining resources. And so, we have reached the end of the road in our technological strides. There is no need to proceed further. Nor is there any reason to continue the arms race. With our present stockpile, we have all the ammunition we need to put an end to all that exists.

Whatever wars accomplished in the past might also have been achieved by peaceful means. The same holds true today. We do not have to destroy each other in order to come to terms with our differences. But war has always been considered the most effective way to deal with any infringement on economic, territorial, or human rights. Therefore, as long as we continue to plan and prepare for war and build up arsenals of armaments, we can expect to become involved in some form of conflict. The problem now is how to limit the escalation of these aggressions to keep them within the realm of resolving the disagreement that exists.

In the past, fighting a war was a difficult and complex operation. Transportation was very hazardous and slow; troop movement was a major concern in starting an encounter; weapons were not mass produced and the number for each battle was limited; food was not easily available, thus soldiers frequently went hungry; weather conditions were often the cause for curtailing action. Fighting was generally limited to a series of battles interspersed with periods of inactivity. The hostilities often continued over a period of many years. The end result rarely justified the human suffering entailed. Today, we can move troops anywhere in the world without inflicting hardship on those involved; food and clothing are easily available; our vast supply of weapons far exceeds our need in this area. However, we are no better able to solve our disputes through armed conflicts than were the armies of the past. We have even less of a chance of reaching an amicable peace, as we often do not know why we are involved in hostilities. We enter into a war, not for any reasons of self-preservation, but as a way of showing our superiority as a nation. Wars are no longer fought to protect homes, families, and territorial domain; they have become a testing ground for military supremacy. What was once a battle to preserve a country's independence has been turned into a power play between nations that has nothing to do with human rights. This willful destruction of innocent people as a show of strength is against all the teachings of our various ethnic codes of honor. War as a means of settling disputes is no longer a viable tool; the risk is far too great. We must begin to seek out alternate ways to deal with our differences.

The major powers of the world would be far better off if they were to give up their efforts to produce more sophisticated nuclear weapons and, instead, combine their intellectual capabilities to find a peaceful means for resolving international unrest. All the time and energy that went into the creation of nuclear weapons might well have been diverted into solving the problems of the people of the world who are in need of life-sustaining measures. The same intellect that was utilized for these destructive purposes should now be made available to establish a world organization to maintain peace. We do have the United Nations and it is a step in the right direction. However, it is not the answer to all of our present-day problems.

The United Nations was established for the purpose of preserving international peace. The organization was officially voted into being on October 24, 1945. Its name was the suggestion of

Franklin D. Roosevelt, then President of the United States. The basic purposes and principles as written in the original charter are:

To MAINTAIN international peace and security;
To DEVELOP friendly relations among nations;
To COOPERATE internationally in solving international economic, social, cultural, and humanitarian problems, and in promoting respect for human rights and fundamental freedom;
To BE A CENTRE for harmonizing the actions of nations in attaining these common ends.

The UNITED NATIONS acts in accordance with the following principles: It is based on the sovereign equality of all its MEMBERS. All MEMBERS are to fulfill in good faith their CHARTER obligations. They are to settle their international disputes by peaceful means and without endangering peace, security, and justice. They are to refrain in their international relations from the threat of use of force against any other STATES. They are to give the UNITED NATIONS every assistance to any action it takes in accordance with the CHARTER, and shall not assist STATES against which the UNITED NATIONS is taking preventive or enforcement action. The UNITED NATIONS shall ensure that STATES which are not MEMBERS act in accordance with these principles insofar as is necessary for the maintenance of international peace and security. Nothing in the CHARTER is to authorize the UNITED NATIONS to intervene in matters which are essentially within the domestic jurisdiction of any STATE.

Membership of the UNITED NATIONS is open to all peace-loving nations which accept the obligations of the UNITED NATION'S CHARTER and, in the judgment of the ORGANIZATION, are able and willing to carry out these obligations. Members may be suspended or expelled by the GENERAL ASSEMBLY on the recommendation of the SECURITY COUNCIL. They may be suspended if the SECURITY COUNCIL is taking enforcement action against them or expelled if they persistently violate the principles of the CHARTER. The SECURITY COUNCIL can restore the rights of a suspended MEMBER STATE.

The GENERAL ASSEMBLY is the main deliberative organ of the United Nations and is composed of all the MEMBER STATES. It has the right to discuss and make recommendations on all matters within the scope of the charter. It has no power to compel action by any GOVERNMENT, but its recommendations carry the weight of world opinion.

It is to be noted that the extent of the UNITED NATIONS authority is to study, suggest, initiate, consider, and supervise, but it has no authority to take action. In the realm of its present jurisdiction, the organization is able to offer assistance in time of a natural disaster. Why should it not also be able to assist in time of a man-made assault against another country's territorial domain? We only need to expand its powers to take action, as needed, to prevent infringement on individual rights on an international level.

Unfortunately, the UNITED NATIONS has not met with much success. Kurt Waldheim, former SECRETARY GENERAL to the UNITED NATIONS, said in his 1980 report on the work of the organization, "As the UNITED NATIONS marked its thirty-fifth anniversary, it has many reasons for anxiety. There is a growing uncertainty and lack of direction on many levels of international society. This is reflected in the deteriorating relationships of some of the more powerful nations, in the continued deadlock on vital economic matters, in the persistence of certain regional conflicts to the detriment both of the peoples concerned and of the wider international community, in humanitarian disasters stemming from political military conflict, and in increasing incidence of politically motivated violence and terror.

In this confused climate, the pursuit of many of the great objectives proclaimed in 1945 may seem to have lost momentum or to have been obscured, while some of the progress made in the last 30 years has been dissipated. A reliable system of international peace and security – the central theme of the CHARTER of the UNITED NATIONS - has developed little further in practice than haphazard and last minute resorts to the UNITED NATIONS. Disarmament, for all meetings and mechanisms, seems a more distant goal than ever, and the world still lives in the shadow of nuclear destruction. The new international economic order remains little more than an abstraction, while the economic prospects of the vast majority of countries and peoples continue to be affected by the general disorder and malaise. Fundamental questions of human rights have been set aside or deadlocked by political and economic expediency. The development and observance of international law and a universally accepted code of international behavior have sustained a series of reverses."

The intent and purpose of the United Nations is admirable; its lack of success is mankinds' great loss. This does not mean that such an organization cannot succeed in the future. We must make a conscientious effort to build upon the foundation already established so that all men will live free from fear of attack by another country and be protected from any aggression that might occur. It should not be necessary for each and every country to maintain a large army, stockpile weapons, and spend huge sums of money on national defense. One world organization could be responsible for taking the necessary peaceful measures for intervening in a crisis situation. Every country should be represented in such an undertaking, none should be denied admittance because of their political beliefs. The goal of the organization should be to maintain international peace, not to convert all nations to one political way of life.

We, as a nation, have no need to undertake the task of saving the world or of setting ourselves up as a super-power in order to force others to do our bidding. No one country can be expected to be responsible for protecting another. It will take the combined efforts of all the countries to solve the problem of aggression. However, we can endeavor to set an example that others might want to follow. On an individual basis, we can refuse to be employed in jobs that are in any way related to the production of nuclear armaments. Without the necessary manpower, these plants will have a difficult time continuing their operation. We can also vote against any measures set forth to allocate funds for defense spending. Another chapter deals with the way in which all American citizens are able to play a role in determining the manner in which their tax dollars are to be utilized. At this time, it is sufficient to point out the methods that might be adapted to alleviate the further production of nuclear weapons. We have created a monster, and before it destroys us, we had best see to its destruction.

With the curtailment of funds for defense spending, the government will have to cease in its effort to create more nuclear weapons. Still, the stockpile will remain and we must seek out ways to eliminate this buildup of nuclear armaments. It will in all probability require a national mandate to convince the powers that be to take such action. We cannot be expected to give up our nations' security. Without these reserves, we are vulnerable to attack by our enemies. We must protect our homeland. We must protect the citizens of our country. Hence, the arguments for its preservation will continue. Actually, a decision to terminate the stockpile will be easier said than done. How to dissipate all of the energy involved without flooding the atmosphere with deadly poisons will call for as an extensive amount of research and ingenuity, on the part of the experts, as was necessary to initially create the atom bomb. What man can put together, he should be able to disassemble. The challenge will be one destined to save our planet; a far more rewarding task than the original endeavor to bring about the means of its destruction.

One does not buy a hand gun unless he intends to use it; even though he may say that it is only to ward off an offender. There is always the possibility of a situation arising that will cause him to use it for other than just a threat. He may unnecessarily injure or take the life of another individual. If it were not available, he would, no doubt, find other means of dealing with his aggressive nature. What we do not have, we cannot use. The same holds true on a national level. Once our country no longer possesses an arsenal of nuclear weapons, it will no longer be in a position to trigger a nuclear holocaust. Only then can we expect to negotiate for similar action to be taken by other nations.

In giving up all nuclear armaments and reverting back to the way of life before the creation of the atom bomb, we will in no way be endangering our national defense. If we were to use our present available supply of nuclear weapons against another country, the retaliation would be immediate. We would suffer just as much as we would if we had no such ammunition available, but were instead the victim of a nuclear attack. Any country initiating such an action would derive no benefits to further its cause. There would be no spoils to carry home, no land to overtake, no prisoners of war to enslave for their own purposes. All they might realize, as a result of their aggression, would be the possibility of the fallout settling over their own country causing them to be the victims of their own nuclear attack.

No country wants to be responsible for starting the final war of the world, but we are coming so close to this as an actuality that it behooves us all to take a stand for our own survival. So, as we come to the end of the twentieth century, let us set our sights on finding peaceful solutions to all of the problems that beset us. Let us spend our time, effort, and money in pursuit of this goal. If we, as a country, have the courage to take the initiative in such an endeavor, we will be able to command the respect of all of the people of the world. We will become the super-power we so earnestly desire to be; not because we are a threat to others, but because of our desire to take the lead in the cause of peace.

We must start to honor the peacemakers of the world, rather than those who lead troops into battle. Once we cease to make heroes of the men who fight wars and pay tribute to the people who work to keep the world a haven for peaceful coexistence, we will be taking a step towards the realization of our goal. True, we do have the Nobel Peace Prize for the encouragement of men and women who work for the betterment of humanity. It was established by the will of Alfred Nobel, the Swedish inventor of dynamite, who died in

1896. He left his entire estate for this purpose. The prizes, averaging $40,000 each, were first awarded in 1901. They are bestowed annually for what is regarded as the most important work during the year in physics, chemistry, medicine or physiology, idealistic literature, and service in the interest of peace. The latter, unfortunately, is all too often granted for ideals that are deemed worthy, rather than for accomplishments that have already been made.

In our own lives, we can plan to avoid conflict or to use it as a way of dealing with life's problems. We can either resolve our differences by a discussion of possible solutions or with a threat of force. The passive solutions harm no man, the forceful threats are often a source of future aggression. We would all be wise to begin to practice peaceful means for settling our personal disputes and to carry out this policy in all areas of our lives.

There is only one road that will lead to the salvation of mankind and it is not the one that we have been traveling. There does not seem to be any hope if we continue on as we are. It is not a question of do we want to take the necessary action, but where should we start? It is a matter of how long we can delay before we reach the point of no return. There is still time to reverse our course, but it is running out. And when it does, we will no longer have a choice. We have nothing to lose by any action we initiate. Why, then, should we hesitate to take a stand? We can never achieve what we do not set out to accomplish.

Chapter Eight
Technological Disaster

Man has always prided himself on his technological achievements. Since the beginning of the twentieth century, he has taken his greatest steps forward. Major advances have been made in the fields of science, medicine, industry, and in the improvement of our living conditions. We no longer depend upon ourselves for our survival, but, rather, on the technological "know-how" that has created the world we now inhabit. We would not want to revert back to the times of our ancestors. We love all of our modern conveniences and our newfound freedom from responsibility. None of us can truly understand what life was like before the advent of electricity. A blackout in New York City in 1965 gave those who experienced it some idea. It was the cause of immediate panic; to be thus deprived of their creature comforts was most certainly an unwelcome and unpleasant situation.

At 5:28 P.M., on November 9, 1965, New York came to a standstill. Eight million people were suddenly immobilized when a power failure engulfed the city. For those watching the Manhattan Skyline from across the Hudson River in New Jersey, New York just disappeared, as lightbulbs flickered and then dimmed to darkness. It seemed like the end of the world to 850,000 commuters trapped in unlighted subway trains that died on their tracks; 17,000 were passengers on four trains that stalled above the East River on the Williamsburg Bridge. Hundreds of elevators were suspended between floors, leaving people restrained like animals in a cage. Inbound airlines to John F. Kennedy Airport remained stacked in the clouds, as the airport lost its runway lights and radar. One thousand travelers, seat-belted for take-off, spent the night in parked planes. All over New York, commuters slept in emergency bedrooms; in makeshift sleeping bags at Grand Central Station; on ships docked in the Hudson River; in the showroom of the Simmons Mattress Company; in

Macy's Department Store furniture department; and at the Park Avenue Armory. Inconveniences and tragedies abounded. At New York hospitals, human assembly lines delivered trays to patients when the elevators stopped. Fifty million pieces of mail clogged the New York Post Office. Food spoiled in warm refrigerators. Many accidental deaths were reported. It was an experience to remember, but not one that anyone would care to endure on an on-going basis.

Incidents such as the blackout in New York City tend to increase our appreciation of our present way life, but still we are not satisfied. We seek to continue to advance our technology on all fronts. We have computerized our industry to the point of almost eliminating the need for human participation in certain areas of endeavor. We look forward to the mass production of a robot that will take over even more of our household chores. We pay tribute to those men and women who, through their efforts to create a human test tube fetus, are supposedly advancing the cause of mankind. We honor any breakthrough as a great and glorious achievement.

We have come so far in our pursuit of knowledge that we now believe it possible to create a super-race by means of a process known as "cloning" – the creation of life through the selection of genes, in order to predetermine the resulting characteristics of an individual. Only the most desirable traits of man will be selected for this purpose. We may someday be a nation of blue-eyed, blond, intellectual giants who will be even better able to further the cause of scientific research. But to what avail? Some of the less desirable world leaders of the past envisioned their countries as being comprised of such a super-race. Fortunately, the scientists have not been too successful in their cloning efforts. They would be wise to set aside such research. A society made up of people of one level of intelligence would soon destroy itself. There would be no one to perform the menial tasks, to comfort and nurture in times of illness or accident, to have an understanding and concern for the preservation of the creatures of the earth and the environment. Who knows what kind of a monster might be turned loose if this practice were put into universal use?

We seem to have lost sight of the true meaning of life and have failed to live up to the time-honored conditions set down for living in accord with each other and with our environment. All the brain power in the world cannot save the human race. What is needed is a universal desire to put an end to further technological advances and a return to a way of life in which respect for our natural resources is of prime concern. We have no need to pursue these exploits into the unknown. We are delving into areas that are not ours to explore, or to know. We may end up by opening Pandora's Box and live to regret the indiscretion.

To travel beyond the confines of our own planet is to enter a sphere of the Universe that is beyond our territorial rights. We have become so egotistical that we think all we have to do is raise the American flag on another planet in order to become the owners of that portion of the Universe. What fools we mortals be! We would fare better if we were to put our efforts into restoring our own allotted space. We are on the verge of destroying the Earth on which we live. It may be nice to visit the Moon, but it will not be so nice there is no place to which we can return. As a nation, we must come to terms with what is rightfully within our realm of responsibility. If there is life on other planets, so let it be! We have survived without this knowledge since the beginning of time and our continued existence is in no way dependent on such factual information. Our country has not benefited from becoming involved in the affairs of other nations. Why should we want to become concerned with the happenings on other planets? Assuming that they are inhabited, what makes us think that we would be welcome? Before too long, we would be telling "these folks" how they could improve conditions in their sphere of influence. The fact that they may be milennium of years older than we are would never be a consideration. We are always good at giving advice, whether or not it has been requested.

The manpower, money, and natural resources that are now used for our technological advances should be converted to more useful endeavors that would put our homeland back into a life-sustaining condition for all of its inhabitants. We may as well face the fact that we have gone too far in our pursuits and forego any future forays into the unknown. We claim to be entering into all of this technological and scientific research for the benefit of future generations, but what we are actually doing is depleting this planet of the very resources that they will need for their survival. What good will these advances do if the human race is no longer around to reap the rewards of our progress? In the meantime, those of us who are inhabiting this space are being deprived of our right to a fruitful existence due to the greed for acclaim on the part of the few who think only in terms of their own desire to break through the barriers that have been established to protect us from self-destruction.

We are not the first of civilized man to reach such great heights in our pursuit of knowledge. Other civilizations have also made great strides, only to collapse and die. There seems to be a point of no return and we are not in any better a position to go beyond this pinnacle than were our predecessors. Take, for example, the city of Pompeii. Once a busy, happy, prosperous metropolis of over 25,000 people, it is now a dead city; where no one has lived for over 2,000 years. During its heyday, Pompeii was the home of wealthy men from Rome who built luxurious seaside villas along the nearby Bay of Naples. In the city itself, there were theatre districts, markets, industrial buildings, elegant homes, temples, a stadium, handsome statues, and an ampitheatre where gladiators slew each other for other men's amusement. Many of the buildings were covered with beautiful paintings and frescoes. Fertile farmlands occupied the fields surrounding Pompeii. It was a clean, efficient city, but it was not destined to survive. In the summer of 79 A.D., Pompeii died suddenly in a terrible rain of fire and ash. Mount Vesuvius, which had remained dormant for centuries, suddenly exploded with a savage violence and a roar that shook the heavens. A fiery column arose, lightning flashed, and the winds roared. Tons of hot ash fell on Pompeii, along with blazing cinders and stones that smashed rooftops and covered the streets. A peaceful day was turned into a wild, burning holocaust. When the eruption ceased, Pompeii was no longer visible; it had been entombed and perished in a single day. Thus it remained until 1748. At that time, a group of workmen digging a canal across the area uncovered buildings and streets. This was the first sign of the lost city. In 1763, the Italian Government took on the excavation of Pompeii and the work has continued since that time. Today, the city stands; the most complete relic in existence.

Another great city that met its doom with stunning rapidity was Crete. Some of its buildings were as large, or larger, than those we build today. Excellent roads criss-crossed its terrain. The Kings' palace was the size of Buckingham Palace in England. The architectural complexity of this structure was awesome. It was well-lighted, well-ventilated, and had sanitary facilities that included drains, ventilators, and conduits for water. Everything was designed for beauty, comfort, and luxury. Bathrooms were splendid. Wonderful frescoes decorated the walls, Paintings were done in vivid colors that depicted the Cretans going about life in a very modern way; participating in the theatre, sports, parties, and feasts. Their's was a highly developed culture. The aristocracy enjoyed a multitude of pleasure and amusement. Crete was a world power on a par with Egypt. Then, in 1400 B.C., when Crete was at the height of its power and its splendor was world renowned, a severe earthquake demolished this city. The glory of Crete was no more.

We also have the legends that tell us about Atlantis; a civilization that supposedly had scientific knowledge and technology that surpassed our accomplishments of today. Atlantis is said to have been a prosperous and powerful island that sank into the sea thousands of years ago during a great natural catastrophe. There are those who believe that Atlantis will rise up again. Should they be correct in their assumption, it will probably prove to be much like the re-surfacing of a sunken ship. No life will remain, in any form, to rekindle the spark needed to revive the city. There will be skeletons of structures and perhaps some treasures and artifacts to give us an idea of the cultural achievement and technological knowledge that was prevalent at that time, but that is about all that will endure. Any lesson to be learned will probably be for us to do all in our power to keep history from repeating itself.

It should be quite obvious that limitations have been set for mankind, that we would be wise to accept these boundaries and learn to live with what has been allowed for our realm of experience. To go beyond may very well lead to our annihilation. We have seen what can happen; however, a repetition of such devastation might not be confined to one city. In today's times, it might become the loss of the entire planet for life-sustaining purposes.

If we can come to terms with living our lives without planning for ways to change the very basic concept of creation, to remain within the confines of that which is ours to enjoy, and to learn to respect the laws of the Universe, we will be heading in the right direction. We will then be able to continue to survive on this Earth and reap the God-given benefits of our natural resources. We cannot improve upon the plan that has already been established for man's continuing existence. Any changes that we make will not, in the final analysis, prove to be any way superior. In time all of our technological advances will turn into technological disasters that we will wish we had never developed. We must realize that the Creator is a great deal smarter than we are and if we let well enough alone, all will be well. The inhabitants of the Earth survived with the natural elements available to them since the beginning of time. What makes us think that we cannot do so now? Are we so brazen as to believe that we are better engineers than the One who developed the overall plan for this planet? We must stop misusing our natural resources in an effort to play God's role in the Universe. We should count our blessings rather than constantly try to change what is into something we consider to be better. As you look around and view the wonders of nature, how can you doubt that there is a master plan for the Universe?

The ways of mankind are very difficult to comprehend. It is understandable that we all want to have comfortable homes, adequate clothing, enough food, and some means of enjoying our leisure time. This is all that should be required to keep us satisfied with life. We should be content with limiting our research to those areas that will enable all men to have an adequate supply of the things necessary to meet these basic needs. However, we are not fulfilled with this as our role. We seem to feel that we must always seek that which is beyond our grasp. We strive to reach new heights, in all fields of endeavor, without ever assessing the value of such achievements, or the havoc they may wrought. We think that unless we push farther and farther into the unknown, we are not living up to our human potential. To merely enjoy life on a day-to-day basis is too little to expect for ourselves. Thus, we strive to achieve and achieve. We see no end to what we might accomplish, but an end is inevitable. It is not the end that we would choose. We must stop all of this useless pursuit of scientific and technological advancement and settle down to enjoy what we have before there is nothing left to enjoy. We must face up to this fact, accept it, and then act in accordance with the kind of commitment it involves.

The technological advances of the past decade in space travel, nuclear experimentation, and scientific research, have in no way improved our quality of life. However, they have caused us to be less able to meet our daily needs because we are paying for all of these projects through our tax dollars. The latter could be put to more valuable use than the pursuit of "green cheese".

Not only is our technology bringing us to the brink of a moral crisis, it is also leading us to the brink of an economic disaster. Why, then, do we sit idly by and fail to discourage such endeavors? We should be very vocal in our disapproval and make known our desire to have these activities curtailed immediately. We must not make heroes of the people who participate in such projects; nor should we even acknowledge their continued efforts. Without the glory, their attempts would soon falter. Why go to the Moon if it is not reported in the news media? It is hardly worth the time, energy, and risk involved if nobody is going to praise the person who undertakes such a mission. Those who devote themselves to these achievements should be looked down upon by society. We would be wise to practice the subtle art of "shunning" as a means of showing our disfavor.

Shunning – not speaking to an individual, thereby showing scorn for his behavior – is an old Amish custom that dates back to 1693. At that time, Jacob Ammain, a Mennonite preacher in Bern, Switzerland, began to emphasize stricter enforcement of Mennonite customs. He especially stressed the doctrine of shunning errant members of the sect. "Meiding", as it is also called, is one of the earliest ritualized community-wide forms of passive control over a member's behavior and it is a most effective form of discipline.

Once we come to terms with what is happening to us as a nation, we will be better able to see the need for a change in our priorities. We must reassess our basic values and make them known to those who are in a position to take a stand against furthering useless causes. We must all begin to realize that there is a way that our lives are meant to be lived. When we suffer from famine and droughts, it is because we have not respected what has been given to us to use for our well-being. There is no doubt that there are adequate resources for all of the inhabitants of this planet. As long as we leave things in their original state, we will all have an opportunity to share in these God-given gifts. There is sufficient water to keep the land lush and the people and the wildlife from perishing from thirst. We may have to dig to find it and to pipe it to our area of concern, but that is all that is required for us to meet this need. We see the animals, the birds, and the creatures of the waters living in their natural habitat with an abundance of the things needed for their survival. They do not try to change their environment. So it should be for mankind. If we cease to go beyond the perimeters set for us, we, too, can enjoy a life of abundance.

We consider ourselves superior to the rest of the animal kingdom. But are we? We might very well take a lesson from them in how to live and let live. The only problems they have are created by mankind who, because of his greed and man-made needs, usurps their natural habitat. Our technology is not only disastrous to us, it is also a crime against the creatures of the land who have equal rights with us on this planet. We make no provision for their escape from our sandblasting equipment as we force them out of areas that they have established for their own use. There is much construction that is needed in order for us to live with all of our creature comforts and to care for our human needs. However, those that in no way benefit us in our day-to-day living must be eliminated. To continue to pursue our technology at the expense of the survival of the other inhabitants of this planet is a disgrace that we can no longer tolerate. Once we face the fact that all of these problems are of our own making, we can begin to rectify our mistakes.

We are all God's children. We are not His architectural engineers. We are not the creators of life. We are not the owners of the Universe. We are a miniscule part of a vast and glorious creation. Let us all respect our role in the scheme of things and give thanks for what has been given, accept it as our due, and ask for no more. There is no other way that we can hope to overcome our present state of impending disaster and enjoy a peaceful and happy existence.

Chapter Nine
The Bureaucratic Nightmare

Periodically, our national government announces plans to put an end to unncessary bureaucratic spending and thereby do away with this monumental waste of the taxpayers money. Good intentions do prevail and hope is generated. However, to date, nothing has been accomplished and the bureaucratic nightmare remains with us. Rather than curtailing expenses, they continue to escalate. This is one of the greatest problems that exist in our government today and it is a constant drain on our economy.

In return for this great expense, little or no good is done in the line of service to the general public. Money is often spent for equipment that is neither needed nor of any value to the organization as a whole. Duplication is rampant, replacements are frequently made before the existing equipment has lost its newness. It is almost a game among politicians to see who can spend the most money on refurbishing their offices. Redecorating is done to suit the whim of the newest tenant. The time involved in designing these changes, as well as the goods and services rendered, is paid for by the taxpayers, who might prefer to spend their hard-earned dollars on redecorating their own homes, but are never given the choice.

It is time to call a halt to these useless expenditures. Offices should be repainted and refurbished on a .time schedule in keeping with normal wear and tear. Furniture, rugs, and equipment should be replaced on a predetermined basis. For example: painting could be done every two years; office equipment replaced every five years; rugs, draperies, and casual furniture replaced every eight years. A new employee, taking over a government office, could personalize it with his own accessories. There is no need to make any other changes in order for the occupant to feel comfortable in his environment. Once a schedule is established, bids could be submitted for the services as needed, and contracts granted to the lowest bidder who meets the required specifications and standards. The completed project should not be paid for until it has been approved by a competent person who has no vested interest in the undertaking.

Another area that requires investigation is the amount of money being spent for office supplies in each individual government agency. This is a very vulnerable spot for waste and pilfering. Any effort to cut expenses should take into consideration ways to eliminate these conditions. There is no need to stockpile large quanitities of supplies. Quotas for each item used should be determined on a monthly basis, then multiplied by twelve to ascertain the amount to be purchased annually. At the end of the fiscal year, those in charge should be held accountable for any existing shortages of these supplies.

Recycling of some items is worth consideration; e.g., discarded computer cards can be utilized in a new manner – some government agencies sell them to paper salvage companies; scrap paper can be saved and used where the finished product is not subject to inspection; many other areas of conservation are also possible, but they differ in each individual operation. Monetary rewards should be offered to employees who recommend acceptable ways to practice economy measures and a system of recognition devised for offices that successfully cut back on the amount of supplies used. Our goal must not be to penalize government employees, but rather to include them in a plan to improve conditions. An incentive system will always bring results; it makes individuals a part of the whole scheme and challenges their ingenuity.

Measures must also be taken to resolve the problem of duplication of services that now exist in local, state, and national agencies. It is far better to deal with issues at the local level where input is available and results can be evaluated. The whole process is less time consuming and it is, therefore, less expensive to provide the necessary services. What can effectively be dealt with locally should not be repeated at the state or national level. The responsibilities of the Federal Government, as defined in Section VIII of The Constitution, relate primarily to Foreign Affairs, the National Budget, National Defense, Interstate Commerce, and to "make all laws which shall be necessary and proper for carrying into execution the foregoing powers." All other concerns should be the responsibility of state and local governments. At the state level, what is not a legislative or judicial matter should be passed on to local governments. Each community understands its own needs and major concerns and is, therefore, better able to institute appropriate measures. Guidelines should be established for certain programs; e.g., unemployment compensation, welfare, and medical assistance, that are applicable to all geographical areas.

One of the most challenging problems we are going to have to be concerned with is the elimination of those agencies that duplicate the services of another. How to decide which one to maintain and which one to discontinue will be a very difficult task. It would be advisable to ask for a Statement of Purpose from each agency in your local community, as well as information as to the number of clients served and the cost of this service on a per-diem basis. Any agency that is operating with federal, state, or local funds will have to reply to such a request if it is made by a responsible body of community-minded people. You may need the backing of a service organization in order to undertake such a task; e.g., the United Way, the Chamber of Commerce, the Junior League, etc. A study will then have to be made of the need for the service rendered and whether or not it is in keeping with the stated purpose of the agency. Those that are most effective in their programs and who are able to maintain their operation at the least cost should be given a stamp of approval. Those who do not live up to their stated purpose and whose operating costs are excessive should be eliminated. If two agencies, offering the same kind of program, are operating with equal effectiveness, they should consolidate. Each will want to keep its own identity and will offer many reasons as to why they are the most essential. Nevertheless, using one facility instead of two as the base of operation will cut overhead costs. We are not obligated to fund every agency that seeks to stay in business. If their services are not needed, or if they are not being efficiently run, we have every right to recommend their termination. Whether the money for their operation comes from local, state, or federal funds, they are still being financed by the taxpayer's dollars.

The sooner we begin to demand an accountability of all bureaucratic operations and bring about a reduction in spending in this area, the sooner our tax dollars can be put to use where there is a need to overcome human deprivation. It may also be the beginning of a lowered tax structure; a blessing that will be worth all the effort it takes to bring about the necessary changes. The end result could be heartwarming for the vast majority of our countrymen.

How are we going to make all this happen? We need only reflect on how changes have been wrought in the past. We women have always been a very strong force in initiating reforms; there is no reason why we cannot now take the lead in a crusade to rectify these existing conditions. We can organize in our own communities and start, on a small scale, to outline what must be done in our immediate area to affect a saving in the operation of local administrative offices and agencies. Each country, township, and borough operates in a fashion that is unique; there is no one way that is applicable for all to follow. It will require a review of what is being done before changes can be recommended. We can enlist the aid of local newspapers to call attention to any duplication of services, or misuse of public funds. There will be very few who will not favor the elimination of unnecessary spending that is depriving them of their ability to care for their own needs. Those who are the recipients of these needless expenditures may rise up in protest, but they will be in the minority. It will be our responsibility to point out the error of their ways and the need for change in the method of conducting their operations. Their subsequent cooperation, or lack of such, should then be given media coverage.

Once we have met with some success in bringing about reforms at the local level, we will have more confidence in our ability to be effective at the state level. The process will be the same. Here again, we will have to seek out any misuse of public funds and demand some form of accountability. Just as local governments all differ in their method of operation, so it is with the fifty states that make up our nation. Each one will have to be dealt with individually. It will only be by a careful review of the status quo that we will be able to ascertain a priority basis from which to begin our campaign. We may find it easier to work through our elected officials; to charge them with this task in their area of responsibility.

We will find it easier to police local and state operations than those at the national level. Once again, our elected officials will have to be prevailed upon to assist us by seeking out ways to cut down on unnecessary spending and recommending the elimination of those bureaucratic creations that are of little or no value. As agencies annual budgets are submitted for approval, they must be carefully scrutinized to ascertain what percentage of their expenses are allocated for services rendered as opposed to those apportioned to management costs. Agencies that are top heavy in favor of management should be cut back or eliminated. Those that do not offer services relating to human needs or environmental protection should be phased out. These cutbacks will result in increased unemployment, but it will be well worth the cost of the unemployment compensation entailed to be freed from the continued waste of money for non-essential bureaucratic indiscretions. The services of the people who are eliminated can soon be diverted to more useful purposes.

The creation of a multiplicity of bureaucratic agencies has been a serious mistake on the part of our national government. Rather than helping, problems have been created that previously did not exist. Uncle Sam cannot be all things to all people and should not attempt to play this role. The network of bureaus, agencies, and offices is so widespread that many do not even know that the other exists, or what their purpose might be. Some employees are not even given a job description and so muddle through each day, trying to act as if they are needed in order to draw a paycheck for which they give nothing in return. Some even boast of their free ride and have no qualms about taking the taxpayer's money. Other may feel some guilt but do not speak out because they are afraid of losing their present financial security.

We cannot sit idly by and let this situation continue. We must take a stand for reform and continue to be heard until some changes are made. Talk is easy, but action is what brings results. We would be wise to start on an intensive campaign to inform those in public office of our desire for immediate action. We will have to flood the mails with letters and telegrams demanding that cuts in spending be made and steps taken to eliminate any duplication of services. Those elected officials who do not heed our requests must not be re-elected and given another chance to lead us further into the economic downhill slide that we are trying to overcome. We are not going to become the victims of a national bankruptcy. We have fought for our rights in the past and we will do so again.

Moderation in government spending is as necessary as moderation in any other area of our lives. It is always the key to successful living. We fail to realize that this premise applies to each and every one of us, in all of our endeavors. No man is excluded; no government operation is free to usurp this as their prerogative and to feel exempt from such limitations. Of late, we have chosen to elect men of great wealth to high public offices. Men who have practiced excessive spending in all areas of their lives and who do not know how to live without these excesses. How can we expect them to understand the value of a uniform plan of money management in the overall operation of the government? Each and every bureau and agency should operate under the same fiscal plan. What is right for one is right for all. Pet projects are not to be granted immunity; nor should valuable social programs be cut in order to allow for excessive spending in other areas. We must not rob the poor in order to increase defense spending. We must not cut our own welfare programs so that we can send arms and ammunition to other countries who are at odds with neighbors. Charity begins at home. We have an obligation to our countrymen that surpasses military aid to other nations.

Our job is to take care of our own people, to provide them with goods and services, as needed. We must forego all areas of international involvement until we have met this obligation on the home-front. Others will survive without our foreign aid; they may even fare better for the lack of it. We have been overplaying our hand in this role while we continue to neglect our own people who are in need.

Our country needs to operate on a balanced budget, but this must not be achieved by allowing for inequities in some areas of national concern. Cutting some programs in order to compensate for excesses in spending in others will never be the answer to our present economic problems. A balanced budget must mean a balance in the distribution of funds, not just two equal figures at the bottom of the asset and liability columns.

We need public officials who have an understanding of this need. Men who will set an example of moderation in their personal lives. Men who have the same dedication to the principles on which this country was founded as those who wrote the Constitution and the Declaration of Independence. We must balance the inequities that now exist; a free ride for some while others remain immobilized is not our national goal. Equality for all must once again surface. Only a practice of moderation in all areas of government spending and a strong resolve on our part to maintain this condition will bring this to fulfillment.

Chapter Ten
"All That Glitters Is Not Gold"

We have reached a point in our history as a nation where material wealth is the standard by which we are most apt to judge ourselves and others. Little value is placed on the good that man does for his fellow man. The number of cars parked in one's driveway is of more importance than the hours spent in giving service to others. We have come so far in our greed that we allow our neighbor to starve while we stockpile food which we may not even be able to utilize. We seem to have forsaken each other in our quest for monetary gain. "Love thy neighbor" carries with it the condition that he must first adhere to our lifestyle and meet our standard of living. Self-worth has been replaced by monetary worth; with no concern being shown as to the manner in which one's funds are acquired.

There seems to be no end to our desire to accumulate trivia. We are on a compulsive buying spree that can only lead to our inevitable downfall. Our natural resources are being depleted in an effort to meet this demand for unnecessary commodities. It is all to no avail. We can only eat and drink so much, wear so many clothes, and utilize so many possessions. We must find a place to store all of our acquired "things". We must have a place to display those that will enhance our prestige. We must care for and preserve our prized acquisitions. So much of our time and energy goes into these useless endeavors that we end up scarificing meaningful relationships with family and friends in order to continue working toward our self-imposed goals.

"All that glitters is not gold." Material possessions will never bring us true happiness. It takes the love and respect of one's fellow man to know real joy in living. We must learn to live our lives one day at a time and be content with satisfying our needs on a daily basis rather than stockpiling for the future. It may seem like a very difficult step to take, however, once done it will not only prove to be beneficial to our economy, it will also aid in the conservation of our natural resources. The demand for available supplies will decrease and, thus, allow for a more even distribution of commodities. The end result will be a decline in prices; as the demand for goods and services is lessened, prices are affected in the same manner. We have nothing to lose by taking such measures; we have everything to lose if we refuse to face up to what must be done to overcome the greed that we have allowed to manifest in our lives. We have become slaves to the material world. It is almost as if we have taken to worshiping false gods and idols. We would be wise, instead, to show our appreciation for all that has been granted to us for our survival on this planet by reaffirming our concern for the environment.

Many who have succumbed to such a false set of values have also become trapped by the need for a means of escape from the reality they have created for themselves. They seek to overcome their fears and self-doubts of their ability to achieve their chosen goals, by over-indulgence in alcohol and drugs. Through these measures they can become, in their own eyes, the person they would like to be and temporarily reach the heights to which they aspire. They have put themselves on a merry-go-round; another ride to nowhere is always available. By creating chemical changes in their brains, they can be sure of momentarily fulfilling their dreams. But they are not really living and will never enjoy true peace and happiness until they learn to strike a balance and accept moderation in all areas of their lives as the key to successful living.

The number of alcoholics and drug addicts in our country is on the increase. These people resent all attempts to discourage them in their destructive ways; nevertheless, when their bubble bursts, they expect society to come to their rescue. This is not society's responsibility. They have created their own misery and they alone will have to overcome their individual situations. If their desire to change is sincere, they can do so. We all have free will. How we choose to conduct our lives is an individual decision. Tax dollars should not be spent on expensive rehabilitation centers for these adult addicts. We are under no obligation to provide treatment for the debilitating effects they have brought about by their own self-abuse. Man's inhumanity to his fellow man is not to be taken lightly; however, in this instance, the problem is not one that has been created by our indifference to the needs of others. It has been brought about by over-indulgence, rather than a lack of the means of survival.

Recreation vies with the accumulation of monetary wealth as the number one priority of our times. The more bizarre, the more outlandish the entertainment, the more it is enjoyed. Flashing lights, obscene acts, physical gyrations, are all part of today's scene. Some people live from one party to the next and try to outdo each other in achieving the absurd. We have surpassed all the limits that have been set for human decency and accept such behavior in the name of "losing one's inhibitions," being "free to be me," and "letting it all hang out." Little is left to the imagination; some is even beyond what the average person is capable of imagining. The pendulum has swung so far that there is only one way that it can now go. Certainly we do not want to revert back to the ways of our puritannical forefathers, but there must be a happy medium somewhere in between. To continue on the path that we are now following will only lead to more broken homes, broken bones, and mental instability. We will just have to take it upon ourselves to refrain from participating in such activities, or patronizing those places that offer these deviant forms of so-called pleasure. The purpose of recreation is to provide a way to relax and renew one's energies. It is not meant to destroy a person's ability to function because of total mental and physical exhaustion. The party is about to come to an end for a great many people. The glamour is wearing off and before long there will be nothing more to experience. Those who might still want to continue in the pursuit of erotic pleasures may soon find that they need their money for life-sustaining goods rather than life-distorting activities.

There was a time when the acquisition of material goods did not affect our economy, or contribute to the misuse of our natural resources. They were the days before the technological advances that we now deem necessary to our existence. When we were only concerned with enjoying fancy clothes and fine furnishings for our homes, there was an ample supply for everyone. And so there can be again if we are willing to make the sacrifices necessary to bring our economy and our environment back to its former healthy state. We will not always have to do without the things we enjoy, however, we will have to learn to temper our greed. Moderation will always be the answer to maintaining a balance between man and his natural resources. In the meantime, we must take measures to cut back on our spending and make do with what we have. The days of high fashion will have to be set aside. A few new items, added to our wardrobes each season, should suffice to keep us from feeling dowdy. If we can accept this as a temporary measure, it will not be a hardship. As long as we are all in the same boat, we should not be adverse to wearing last year's model. Those who appear "decked-out" in new attire are the ones who should be made to feel out of step with changing times. We can make a game of resurrecting our old clothes and refurbishing them. A fifteen year old suit or dress worn to a social gathering ought to evoke more praise than the latest fashion design.

Another measure that might be given consideration is the setting up of clothing exchange stations in each geographical area. They would provide an opportunity for the local people to swap their old clothes for others that are "new" to them. They would also benefit those who have undergone a recent weight change and find themselves in need of a different size. A small fee could be charged for each article; with credit being given for items donated. Individuals in each community would, no doubt, devise their own scheme for operating such a venture.

The increased cost of gasoline will continue to cause us to curtail the use of our automobiles for anything that is not a necessity. We will, therefore, be unable to travel far from home for our entertainment. Provisions for recreation should become a community project. We are going to need a lot of outlets for our frustrations as we go through the solution to the problems that beset our country. Rather than sit home alone and indulge in mind-altering escapes, we would be wise to join forces with our neighbors and plan for ways to make the most of what is available to us for leisure time activities. Elaborate parties are becoming past history; increasing food costs make it difficult to feed any additional people. Instead of trying to outdo each other to see who can stage the most gala affair, we should save our accolades for those who plan the most innovative social functions with the overall cost being shared by the participants. "What can I bring?" should be the stock phrase when accepting an invitation to share the hospitality of another's home. This will actually make party-giving more fun, less work for the hostess, and lead to more such gatherings. In the long run, we will probably enjoy life more because of our increased social activity. The alternative is to sit home and bemoan our fate. Rich or poor, we all need and enjoy the company of friends. Some people are more outgoing and friendlier than others, but even the shy and retiring benefit from an association with their peers.

If we are to continue as a nation, we will have to forego all the glamour and glitter of the past decade. Did we even enjoy the debacle? We thought we did, but were we actually any happier for the rat race to nowhere? Did the means justify the end? If we had it to do all over again, would we do it differently? Hindsight provides us with new perspectives. We cannot change what has been done, but we can certainly go about living in a different manner in the future. It may be difficult for some to slow down, change their ways, to accept that less is better, but we are survival-oriented and, in spite of our complaints, we will do what must be done. Those who refuse to cooperate will be at the mercy of their fellow man. No man has a right to be exempt from the steps that must be taken to put our nation back on its feet. The wealthy created more of the problems than the poor; they had best be ready to make amends for their part in our national crisis.

In spite of all the problems that we face, we are still better off than a great majority of the world's population. Once we have successfully dealt with the curtailment of our nuclear, scientific, and technological endeavors, we can forge ahead and put our country in order without sacrificing any of our basic needs. For this we should be grateful. Still, it is going to take cooperation, dedication, and a willingness to deprive ourselves of the non-essentials to which we have become accustomed. Those of us who overeat and gain weight must go on a diet in order to return to our normal size. It is the same with our country. We must cut back in those areas in which we have overindulged in order to bring our economy and environment back to their normal state. There will be lean years ahead but we will all be healthier and happier because of the good that we will be accomplishing. Gradually, we will begin to overcome our present dilemma and once again be able to enjoy a few more luxuries in our daily lives.

It is always helpful to have a time frame in which to operate. It is like being able to see the light at the end of a long tunnel; to know that our immediate situation will not endure forever. It has taken us two hundred years to reach our present state. Let us hope that we can reserve the trend and bring about the necessary changes within the next ten years. It seems like a long time and we may be able to do better, but the wheels of progress often move slowly and we must be prepared to meet with opposition and obstacles along the way.

As we take to our attics to see what we can find to wear to the next gathering of the clan and give away or sell those things that serve no purpose in our lives, we will, undoubtedly, be relieved to forego the competition of maintaining a lifestyle that we can no longer afford. The peace of mind should compensate for the lack of excitement we have come to expect to stimulate our psyches. A slow down is not a shut down, it is just a temporary measure to maintain the status quo, until an upsurge begins anew. We may have to give up the icing on the cake, but as long as we still have the cake we can always ice it at some future time.

There is much in the world that can dazzle our eyes, without emptying our pocketbooks. It is not the splendor of our own creation, but rather the wonders of the natural world around us. We do not have to create our own glitter, it is supplied for us in the heavens above. What sparkling lights can we manufacture that will be more beautiful than the twinkling of the stars? What greater illumination can we provide than the light of the moon on an otherwise dark night? Instead of sitting indoors being captivated by our own inventions, we might begin to study astronomy and the heavenly bodies of the sky. It has far more to offer in the way of intrigue than all the manmade hoopla of the blacklight cult. A beautiful sunset can be far more mind boggling than the psychedelic lighting to which many have succumbed as a way to reach higher states of consciousness. One need only observe the daily display in nature to have a continuing show of unbelievable beauty. Too many of us never take the time to observe these natural wonders. How many have never seen a sunrise or a sunset? The colors that evolve far surpass any that our artists can blend.

A walk though such a place as Longwood Gardens will be more breathtaking than anything man can hope to duplicate. Located in Chester County, Pennsylvania, thirty miles southwest of Philadelphia, it is a kaleidoscope of horticultural beauty. Formal and informal gardens, sparkling fountains and magnificent conservatories, with four acres of plants under glass, make Longwood Gardens a delight at any season, if not each passing day. It covers more than 1,000 acres, with 350 for the display gardens alone, and was developed to its present state by Pierre Samuel du Pont. It is truly one of the most outstanding garden displays in the world, featuring a fountain garden, an Italian water garden, waterlily pools, an All-American rose garden, a wildflower garden, and extensive wooded areas and lakes. The conservatories include the azalea-camellia, rose, desert and palm houses and also displays of bonsai and tropical plants. An orchid display is changed weekly. This bringing together of all the different varieties of flowers and plants under one roof far surpasses all the beauty that we humans can ever hope to create on our own.

To stand and gaze at the ocean as the tide rolls in and out is truly a magnificent sight. It is also a great panacea. All the manmade problems of the world seem to dissipate as one becomes in tune with the movement of the sea.

The view from the highest mountains can bring us to an understanding of man's true place in the universe. Looking down at miniscule houses, cars, and public buildings makes one realize that these creations are not truly a part of the meaning of life. They are for our own convenience – that is all. They should not dominate our lives and turn us into slaves. They are only what we are willing to let them become. It takes the getting away and looking down to make us realize that there is so much more to life than our materialistic pursuits and mind boggling forms of recreation.

As we learn to develop an appreciation of the natural world around us and to take advantage of all that it has to offer, we can begin to let go of our self-imposed limitations and enjoy life as it was meant to be. There is plenty of glitter to add spice to our daily lives without distorting our environment into a grotesque apparition. There is no charge for nature's show; nor are there any debilitating aftereffects. It is all there for us to enjoy, if we will only take the time to do so.

Chapter Eleven
The Cause And Effect Of The Destruction Of Our Environment

There is a lot of unspoiled natural beauty in our country. It serves as a reminder to us of the way the whole planet was at the time of its creation. Gradually, we have destroyed a large portion of this beauty and we are well on our way to finalizing its devastation. Many people become very annoyed when the "environmentalists" raise their voices in protest of such actions. Can't something be done to silence these crackpots? What difference does it make if we eliminate some rare species of wildlife? They are against progress. Roads must be built, nuclear plants must be constructed, dams are vital in certain locations. These are the important things in our lives. We cannot let ourselves be denied the right to forge ahead in our endeavors because of some foolish nonsense about preserving every variety of animal, bird, or fish that exists on this planet. Fortunately, there are a few among us who do have compassion for the creatures of the Earth, and it would be to our advantage to heed the advice of those who foresee the extinction of a great many of these innocent victims of our so-called progress.

For too long a time we have acted as if we owned a portion of the Universe; that the planet on which we live belongs to us; that we can do with it as we please. We have disrupted the natural state of the environment by rearranging the water systems, eliminating trees and forests, and destroying the natural habitat of the wildlife. We have felt no obligation to maintain the Earth in its original state; nor have we felt any responsibility for the negative aspects of our actions. We have expected to do as we please without suffering any ill effects. Man in his folly has been writing the last chapter in the history of his existence on this planet. We are now not only faced with shortages of vital commodities, but also with the pollution of the air, the water, and the food that we eat. We cannot continue to survive if these conditions are not corrected.

We are already beginning to realize the negative effects of pollution on the creatures of the water; many of us have become seriously ill from eating contaminated seafood. These conditions are not going to improve until we stop dumping toxic waste matter from chemical plants and factories into our waters. These same industries are also polluting the air and soon our crops will not be edible because of the rain showers that cover them with toxic matter from the atmosphere. In many of our cities people are suffering physical disorders as a result of air pollution. Diseases of the lungs and respiratory system are on the upswing and will continue to escalate unless some drastic measures are taken to lessen the danger that now exists. If we do not seriously start to make amends for all the harm we have done to our environment, we will soon find ourselves polluting our bodies beyond all hope for recovery. Medical doctors can do a great deal to help us to live free from disease, pain and suffering, but it will take more than scientific knowledge to save us from the debilitating effects of impure food, water and air.

We are also causing our wildlife to be subjected to these same devastating conditions. They are as affected by the environment as we human beings. Not only are we contaminating our own bodies, we are also causing harm to all other living creatures. To continue on with our present disregard for our surroundings will only lead to the eventual destruction of all living matter. How long will the grass remain green, the flowers bloom, the trees bear fruit, if we do not make a conscientious effort to rectify existing conditions?

What measures can we take to overcome this present deplorable state? We will have to establish laws, which are strictly enforced, to prohibit the dumping of unsafe waste into our waters; to control the amount of refuse that may be dumped into a fixed area, so as to keep it within safety standards; and to eliminate the escape of poisonous gases into the atmosphere. Any factories or industries that fail to comply with the established rules of operation must be shut down. Large fines are not the answer as a means of control. In most cases, they will be levied and paid without any improvement in the existing conditions. More drastic action is needed. Workers who are forced out of their jobs should be subsidized for their loss of pay until such time as standards are met and they can return to work. The subsidy should be paid by the federal government, but reimbursement for such expenditures must be made by the offending employer, before the plant in question is permitted to resume its operation.

It, is quite possible that some so-called objectionable refuse might be converted to useful purposes. Much of what we waste may be suitable for recycling and become a financial asset to the industries or factories that have been so freely disposing of all unused materials. With restrictions on dumping, experimentation along these lines is more likely to be undertaken and may provide the solution to a lot of unresolved problems. Even some of the undesirable gases that are escaping into the atmosphere may be tapped and put to a worthwhile use.

There was a time when the air was pure, the water was pure, and all God's creatures thrived on the natural resources around them. Gradually our technology and desire to live in ways that we consider to be superior have brought us to the point of almost certain destruction of all that we have taken for granted as "ours". But no man owns the Earth. It would be better to live as if we were renting a space for a given period of time that is to be returned to its owner in the same condition, or better, than when we originally became the occupant. Let us start to show the proper respect for our landlord and begin to put our small portion of the Earth back to its original state. We do not need all of the chemical and plastic goods that are now being manufactured; nor do we need the nuclear plants that fill the atmosphere with radiation particles. In order to free up our land and restore it to its original purpose, we are going to have to put an end to the production of any unnecessary commodities that play such a large role in the pollution of the environment. It will also be necessary to curtail any further building of nuclear plants and to dismantle and level those that have already been constructed.

We are presently going in circles: we are building plants to create energy; at the same time we are depleting our available supply of energy in order to complete the new construction. The energy that we can save by giving up nuclear experimentation and armament buildup will, no doubt, be sufficient to put us back on the road to recovery. As land is made available, crops can be grown and we can once again reap the benefits of having the produce necessary to feed all of our population. We may even be in a position to assist in alleviating some of the worldwide hunger that now exists. We like to think that we are helping in this area when we make a monetary contribution; however, today's dollars will not buy tomorrow's crops if there are none available because of our misuse of the land. It seems like a monumental task to restore our country to a state of being that will allow all of us to live with an abundance of natural resources that are free from the ill effects of pollution. And it will be a tremendous undertaking, yet it is not an impossible one. We know it can be done because there are those who have already shown us the way.

Picture a quiet rural community where the farmers grow enough food to supply all the residents of the area. Home canning and freezing assures a year-round supply of fruits and vegetables. Livestock is available to provide meat on an ongoing basis. Some of the residents hunt and fish to supply their own needs. Chickens are maintained for a supply of poultry and eggs. Turkeys are always available at Thanksgiving time. Milk and milk products are provided by a local dairy. Home-backed goods are supplied by those who choose to earn their livelihood in this manner. All of these food items can be purchased at the local farmer's market. No one tries to make an enormous profit; they charge just enough to maintain themselves and to pay for their overhead. Greed is an unknown commodity. Some bartering of crops and services is a standard practice.

There is a great respect for the land. The farmers regard the soil as God's property which they work, in trust, during their lifetime. They pride themselves on turning the soil over to their sons in as good a condition as when they received it from their fathers. Many families have lived on the same land for generations and will, undoubtedly, continue to maintain their reputation as the best farmers in the area and their farms as the most fertile in the nation.

Such people really do exist; this is not a hypothetical community. It is a description of the way of life of the Amish and the Mennonites, often referred to as the "Plain People", who reside in what is known as the Dutch Country of Berks, Lancaster, and Chester counties in Pennsylvania. They are a gentle, joyful, intelligent, and delightfully spiritual people whose mere presence is somehow calming. They have been able to maintain their lifestyle and beliefs amid the chaos, confusion, financial struggle, and international problems that plague the rest of the world around them. Their moral values emphasize integrity, honesty, simplicity, and pacifism. They de-emphasize the use of detriments to the human body, mind, and spirit.

The "Plain People" help each other with no thought of any monetary gain. They settle their differences without the aid of law enforcement officers. They ignore our present political system and follow the teachings of their faith. They do avail themselves of the services of the medical profession, as needed, but for the most part, they are healthy and strong. Their mode of dress is simple; they do not adhere to the latest fashion trends. Many still use a horse and buggy as their means of transporation. They practice moderation in all areas of their lives, yet they know no want. They have a great respect for all that abounds in nature and make wise use of their natural resources. They are totally dedicated to remaining self-sufficient within their own communities.

The "Plain People" are able to live with a great deal of peace and happiness in their daily lives. They are not subject to all the adversity that plagues most of the rest of the world. They refuse to participate in any branch of the military service because of their conscientious objection to armed conflict. Still, they do not have total peace of mind because they, too, must face the possibility of an all-out nuclear war. Although they in no way contributed to the creation of the weapons that make it a threat, they are as vulnerable as the rest of mankind to its devastating effects. They cannot change what is happening in the world outside their own insular communities; we are the ones who must alter our course.

Theirs is a way of living that we would all be wise to study. They set an example of what life can be like if materialism is not one's main reason for being. They make us realize that it is possible to have fulfilling lives without all the wanton waste that is prevalent in most of today's society; that there is hope for us and for future generations to be free from want, need, and anxiety. They are a people to be emulated. We may not be eager to change our lifestyle, nevertheless to do so need not be a great hardship. It will not affect our health; cause us to suffer from a lack of any of the basic commodities necessary for our comfort; nor will it put an end to recreational activities and interpersonal relationships. It will, however, be a positive step toward curtailing inflation, reducing our dependency on other countries for essential commodities, improving our environment, and gradually restoring our country to its original state of natural beauty.

In order for this to become a reality, we will first have to start with ourselves and make a commitment to the preservation of our environment. We will not need a soapbox. It will not be necessary to attend rallies and meetings. We do not even have to talk about what we are doing; we only need to do. We must begin today to assume a responsible attitude toward the land, to keep our own space in order, to practice moderation in all areas of our lives,and to refrain from stockpiling for the future. Once we have embarked on our own individual commitment, we can then, by example, influence the other members of our familes to join forces with this effort. Once families start to band together, communities and geographical areas will gradually become involved. Those who refuse to be a part of the movement should be subject to the quiet, passive discipline of shunning.

All of this will not happen overnight, but we can change our ways overnight and start on the road to recovery. Each step of the way will bring us closer to our goal. Who among us can question the reality of this need? Every day the news media brings us reports of more destruction to our environment, increase in disease-related pollution, and increased costs for all of those things needed for our survival. It is a very grim future that we face if we do not take matters into our own hands.

Tomorrow may be too late to start on a plan to bring our country back to its natural state. Some devastated areas are so burnt out that it does not seem possible to restore them. Many sections of our large cities reflect the present decadent way of life to such a degree that one wonders if it is even worth trying to salvage them. What can be done to make the "Times Square" area of New York City a thing of beauty? The squalor that exists there seems to be beyond man's ability to overcome. It will take a bulldozer to remove all traces of the debacle that exists. If this were to take place, it certainly would not be a loss to mankind. This is the attitude of many who remember it in its heyday as "The Great White Way".

Those who now frequent this area on a continuing basis probably have never known a different way of life and have nothing to strive for in the way of self-improvement for themselves or for their surroundings. We cannot miss what we do not know. Habits of a lifetime are hard to break. Yet nothing is impossible if we truly set our minds to its accomplishment. There must be a way to improve conditions in the ghettos of our cities without resorting to destructive measures. We must restore them on a one-step-at-a-time basis. Let us take, as an example, West Forty-Second Street in New York City for the two block expanse between Sixth and Eighth Avenues. The scene is one of prostitutes and pimps, drug addicts, dealers and pushers, alcoholics, sex perversion in all of its ramifications, crime and violence, as well as hunger, poverty and fear. To put an end to these conditions certainly seems like an "impossible dream". Where to begin? How to begin? If we take away the base of operation of those who "hang out" in this area, they will go elsewhere and we will just have two different blocks of the same human dregs. This need not be so! We must start with the premise that we are dealing with our fellow man who has the same basic need for food, clothing, shelter, and recreation as the rest of society. Many of these people have found themselves trapped in a way of life that they do not know how to escape. Some may never make a decision to change but that does not give us cause to lose hope for all. Given a chance, there are many who will mend their ways. Assistance has been offered to these people in the past but it was always something that they had to go to in order to receive the aid. Food and shelter were available but it was somewhere else and their motivation to seek it out was not very strong. It would be far better to bring the help to 42nd Street – the old "Soup Kitchen" routine would be a good start. A hot meal can divert anyone's attention momentarily; the knowledge that it will be available on an ongoing basis might bring hope to an otherwise desperate soul. There should be no strings attached. A month of available, free food would begin to make the "neighborhood gang" feel a little more comfortable and secure. Lack of hope often drives people to accept lifestyles that are harmful and self-destructive. Next a clothing station should be set up to provide for those in need of this kind of assistance; nothing fancy – just articles suitable for the prevailing weather conditions. Once again, this must be given with no strings attached. Finally, emergency shelter should be provided, in the immediate vicinity, for those who are unable to provide for their own housing. After several months of such assistance, the local residents, or frequenters, should be invited to assemble for a civic meeting. One of their own people, with obvious leadership qualities, should be asked to preside at the meeting; the purpose of which will be to enlist aid in refurbishing the area. Nothing is to be said about their habits, lifestyle, forms of recreation, etc. The idea to be presented will be to make their space in the city one that can set an example for others to follow. A general cleanup will be in order. Paint and paintbrushes will be provided to spruce up the buildings. Wooden containers for planting small trees and flowers will be made available. Media coverage will be given to the project. Pride in accomplishment will be stressed, as all labor will be donated. Anyone failing to participate will be at the mercy of his peers. Those who do not contribute will, undoubtedly, be forced out of the neighborhood.

The money spent on such a project will in the end be repaid by the decreased demand for police to patrol the area. It will be self-disciplined by the "locals". There will, of course, be problems along the way; some dissension in the ranks is to be expected; personality problems will arise; human failings will surface. The working through of solutions will be a lesson in living for these folks who have, heretofore, resorted to violence to solve all problems. A committee to arbitrate disputes would be helpful; someone to listen to the fears, doubts, and disagreements that arise. Gradually, the free handouts will cease to be necessary and can be phased out of the picture. Those still in need can seek assistance from the established welfare programs. Hopefully, other folks will get on the bandwagon and join in an undertaking to save their space and restore it to a place in which they can take pride.

There is no need to destroy the environment; to do so will only bring us grief and misery; we cannot derive any benefit from such action. It is as easy to preserve what we have as it is to misuse it. The choice is ours to make. What will your decision be? Are you going to sit back and bemoan your fate as you watch what is left of the natural beauty of the Earth disappear, or are you willing to make a commitment to become involved in improving conditions in your sphere of influence?

Chapter Twelve
A New Beginning

No one will deny that our world is in very serious trouble. It is so bad that we are not certain that there is any hope for the future. It is quite obvious that we cannot go on as we have been; changes are going to have to be made. Still, we are not sure that we can alter the course of man's destiny. After all, the last war of the world is predicted to happen at about this time in the history of mankind. The prediction of the French prophet Nostradamus in 1555 A.D. and the Revelation to John, as recorded in the Book of Revelation in the New Testament of the Holy Bible, are two sources that we are inclined to consider authentic, that have foretold this inevitable fate for the human race. The time for this happening is defined for us in Daniel:12 in the Old Testament. Knowledgeable people are now saying that man will probably not survive this century; pollution, ecological imbalance, and nuclear threats all point to the end of the world.

Those who believe in a literal interpretation of the Bible find all the signs in our present day civilization pinpointed, like stepping stones, to our unavoidable doom. "You must face the fact: the final age of this world is to be a time of trouble; men will love nothing but money and self; they will be arrogant, boastful and abusive; with no respect for their parents." (Paul in II Timothy 3:1,2 New English Bible) In II Peter:2, we are warned to beware of a time when men will despise government, riot in the daytime, speak evil of those in authority, speak swelling words of vanity, seduce the innocent and mock righteousness, laugh at and flirt with evil powers, and proudly boast of their perversion and sin. These very things are now happening all around us and are reported daily by the news media. This should have a sobering effect on all of us; we may very well be the last generation. However, what these literal interpretors fail to consider when they predict the day and time of our inevitable downfall is that when these prophesies were made, our present calendar and clocks were not in existence. Therefore, it would have been impossible to foretell the future in our present time frame. No man can pinpoint the exact time of any event that was written into our history so long ago. We must also take into consideration the fact that these predictions may have been meant to serve as a warning to mankind; as to what the final outcome might be if he failed to live in accordance with the teachings as set down by the prophets.

It may be that we have come to a fork in the road and have one last choice as to which way to go. There is no question as to where one road leads, we have been on it for too long and its destination is becoming more and more obvious. But what of the other road? Certainly it cannot be any more grim a path than the one we are currently following. Possibly, it will be the way to a brighter future. If one road will take us to the predicted end of all that exists for all time, might not the other road open up the way to a new beginning?

Mankind has always recognized the existence of a Supreme Being. This becomes quite obvious as we examine all of the existing religions; there is a God to be found in everyone. For as long as man adhered to his religious beliefs and teachings, his lot was far better than it is at the present time. This is not to say that religion is the answer to all of our problems; nevertheless, the acknowledgment of a force greater than ourselves, with the power to save us from our present self-induced destruction, is certainly worth taking into consideration. We might well heed the advice of the historian, Arnold Toynbee, when he says, "We have turned to conquest of a material nature and, therefore, have become very rich in the material sense. But we are poor spiritually. I think it may be time to turn back in that direction towards religion. I don't mean going to church and reciting certain creeds, the outward form of religion. By religion I mean the inner spiritual form of religion." In order to fulfill such a goal, we will have to be willing to give up our lives to the God of our choice and allow the course of our lives to be dealt with at a higher level. This can best be achieved by living one day at a time and not pondering over what the future might have in store. Or, as it was very aptly expressed in the lyrics from Que Sera Sera, "Whatever will be, will be. The future's not ours to see". This letting go will require a lot of trust as we will no longer be completely in charge of our own lives. It may not be easy but when we consider the alternatives, what do we have to lose?

To accept a Supreme Being as the Protector of the Universe is the first step in freeing ourselves from the present aura of doom that prevails in our society today. For He will most certainly do all in His power to keep His creation from being destroyed. If we work hard to establish a home for ourselves, we are also going to do all that we can to preserve what we have achieved. We may run into a variety of problems or adverse conditions that will be a challenge to overcome, but once we have succeeded in our efforts, we will have a greater appreciation of our own capabilities and a stronger desire to maintain what is rightfully ours. And so it will be for the future of the human race. Once we are willing to put our trust in the Creator, He will do what must be done to preserve mankind and to fight off the evils that beset us in order that we may all live with an increased awareness of our potential for survival.

We have free choice and it will be up to us to either accept or reject the help that is available to us. To refuse to see the light and to follow it to our eventual salvation will leave us with the alternate course of continuing on the insidious path that is currently causing us to live with, or be surrounded by, a great deal of grief and misery. As we begin to show our willingness to change our ways, to alter our course, and to take the risk involved in giving up our destiny to a higher being, we will in all probability see the beginning of the end of the problems that plague us. Certainly it is worth a try. Therefore, when you come to the fork in the road, do not be afraid to take a chance and head in a different direction. If it works for you, others may choose to follow your way and realize that the inevitable prediction of doom is reversible.

We keep looking to others to solve our problems, but we are not looking in the right direction. We must first look to ourselves and decide what we are going to do to improve our own lot. We must make a commitment to change in our own lives. Everything begins with the individual. So start today to re-dedicate your life to a more useful purpose and try to think more positively about the future. Confidence breeds confidence, just as discontent breeds discontent. Once you can face each day secure in the knowledge that you will overcome all of the obstacles it may present, you will begin to live in a more relaxed manner. Do not be concerned about tomorrow, it will soon be the today that you worried about yesterday. Take one day at a time, trust in your ability to cope with its challenges, and enjoy the good that comes your way. As you free yourself from anxiety about the past and the future, you will come to understand the meaning of "casting all your worries aside".

For quite sometime, we have been seeking the kind of leadership needed to guide our country through these difficult times; to bring order out of the chaos, confusion, and uncertainty that exists. To date, we have not found any one person who has a solution to all of the problems that confront us. Those who try to deal with the concerns of our country meet with a great deal of frustration and defeat. Although they have good intentions, they are unable to achieve any degree of success. The task seems to be beyond the capabilities of any one man. To expect to find a person who will resolve all of our difficulties is to dream of a "Prince Charming on a White Horse" who will come and carry each of us to an enchanted island to live forever in peace and happiness. Would that it were possible for such an event to occur so that we could all be rescued from life's trials and tribulations. However, we cannot count on a "Prince Charming" or a "knight in shining armor" to be our saviour. Hopefully, a leader will eventually emerge who will guide our nation to a renewed state, but until that day comes, we are going to have to take matters into our own hands.

There is much that we can do to overcome the mistakes of the past. At present our goals do not include the improvement of conditions for our fellow man, but rather the betterment of ourselves through the acquisition of goods and services that will free us from the need to be involved in anything other than the pursuit of our own pleasure. The rights of the individual have become paramount and supersede all other concerns. We no longer are our brother's keeper. We no longer are the tillers of the soil for the purpose of survival. We have become obsessed with a desire to acquire and acquire and acquire. Whatever we do has a monetary goal with which we expect to buy our way to happiness. Yet our goals are not providing us with a useful and purposeful existence and we are becoming more and more disenchanted with the world in which we live. We are beginning to question the validity of our beliefs. We have reached a point where we do not have the means to acquire more worldly possessions and we are willing to consider making some changes in our ways. But where does one begin?

As a first step, you should take stock of all of your worldly possessions and decide which among them serve no useful purpose. Then, while there are still merchants who are in the business of buying second-hand articles, sell what you are not able to use or enjoy. The extra money can always be set aside for unexpected emergencies. Family heirlooms and treasured works of art should not be disposed of but kept to hand down to your heirs.

Put all of your clothing in wearable condition and sell or give away what you cannot use. Plan to purchase only those items that are necessary to "round out" your wardrobe.

Start a vegetable garden. If you do not have any available land, you may be able to lease a plot from a friend or a relative in exchange for some of the produce that you grow. Plant your garden so that you have a supply of vegetables throughout the spring, summer, and fall. Rotating crops provides for variety, as well as continuity. Home canning and freezing can then become a family project and greatly reduce your food costs on an annual basis.

You will want to take measures to reduce your use of fuel. The oil that is now being taken out of the ground was made by nature millions of years ago. It is not replaced as it is used and the supply is being depleted at a greater rate each year. Sometime in the future it may all be gone – burned up in our furnaces and automobiles. You can save fuel by not overheating your home and by not wasting electricity. Plan the use of your appliances so as to utilize all of their available capacity. Take stock of any areas in your home that allow heat to escape and then make the changes necessary to eliminate these conditions. Any investment you make to reduce fuel consumption will, no doubt, pay for itself in a very short time. During the heating season, shut off rooms that are not in use. In the springtime we rejoice when the temperature reaches 65°; why should we consider it uncomfortable in the winter months? It is just a matter of wearing the proper clothing in order to be comfortable in buildings maintained at 65°.

In the area of transportation, you can save on the use of oil and gasoline by driving no faster than 55 miles per hour; using public transportation when it is available; car pooling whenever possible; walking to any destination that is less than one mile; and using your automobile only when necessary. The more that you can cut back on your use of fuel, the more money you will be saving and the less demand there will be on our natural resources. Each of us will only be responsible for a small savings, but multiplied by millions, the impact should be monumental.

It would be to your advantage to begin today to take stock of your priorities and to set down those that are essential to your well-being. Then list the areas of your life where you are expending unnecessary time and energy. If you are working hard in order to purchase items that you could very easily and comfortably live without, it would be wise to cease to overextend yourself and to settle for what you really need. Once we learn to live with less and to demand less, our lives will begin to change for the better. We will have more leisure time to spend with our families and friends. We will have more money to spend on necessities and the simple pleasures that are available to us for our enjoyment. We will no longer be slaves to our self-imposed need to acquire more than we can use and enjoy. As our lifestyle becomes more basic, our need for financial remuneration will decrease and our workload can be lessened accordingly. No doubt our physical and mental health will improve as the stress factor in our daily living diminishes. There will be more joy in the lives of those who are willing to make these changes.

With a decline in the demand for unnecessary items, more time can be devoted to the manufacture of essential products and more care can be taken with the work that is done. Pride in workmanship can once again be instilled. There will also be a cutback in the number of hours that factories will operate. This will be followed by a reduction in the amount of fuel, electricity, and other natural resources that are currently being used in the mass production of goods. The end result will be a lessening of our dependence on other countries for necessary supplies. Eventually we will become self-sufficient and will no longer be at the mercy of those who threaten to cut off our supply of essential materials if we do not acquiesce to their demands.

The increase in the cost of living over the past decade is causing us all to overspend and, in some cases, to live beyond our means. Until we are willing to curtail all unnecessary spending, it will continue to rise. The law of supply and demand will always control the economy of our country. As the demand for goods decreases, price will begin to decline. The purchasing power of the dollar will increase, and we will be able to live on less income. So, before we cannot afford to survive, let us all start to try to get along with less and, in the long run, we will have more.

If each individual would be willing to start on as simple a campaign as outlined, it could be the beginning of a peaceful revolution that would lead us all to a new beginning. As a woman, I would like to call upon those of my gender to take it upon themselves to begin immediately to instigate changes in their daily living. It is not asking much. It will not deprive anyone of their basic needs. It will only help all of us to live more realistically in a world where reality has become something to escape. Whether or not we are able to overcome all of the obstacles to bring our country back to a semblance of sane living depends on our willingness to do our part. Our children's future is in our hands. If they are to survive, it will be up to us to make their world safe. We must start at once to plan for their legacy. To continue in our present fashion will be futile; the need for change is paramount.

We would all be wise to embark on the course that will lead us to a new beginning. It will not be a difficult route, as the road forges straight ahead, is well marked, and is easy to follow. All we need is the determination to resist the temptation to stray from our chosen path as we journey on our way.

Chapter Thirteen
An End To Government Supremacy

The time has come for all good men to come to the aid of their country; not just to save the environment, although that is a major concern, but also to put the whole political scene in a state of sane and sound operation. We know what is wrong with our government, but until measures are taken to initiate some changes, we cannot expect to see any improvement. Our nation cannot continue to operate as it has been without facing a total financial collapse of the economy. We hear talk about our future armament buildup, our future defense spending, the continued development of nuclear energy, and research to find alternate sources of energy. Consideration is never given to curtailing any of these programs in order to live with what we can afford. We all know the necessity of budgeting in our own lives and realize the pitfalls involved in overspending. Why can't our government officials have the same understanding on a much broader scale? They continue to spend and spend and spend in areas that are not vital to our survival. This waste of manpower, resources, and tax dollars must be brought to a halt for all time. It is not a question of should we? Or how much should we curtail? Or when should we take such action? There is only one answer. ***NOW***, is the time. Just as we must, occasionally, pull in the reins to set our own households in order, we must now begin to take steps to put the affairs of our nation in order.

It would be in our own best interest to start to boycott all unnecessary expenditures of money at every level of government. A look at what is happening in the area of revenue sharing should make us aware of the need for immediate action. Federal funds are being allocated to the states to assist them in meeting their individual needs. The states, in turn, frequently redistribute these funds to their local municipalities to use as they see fit. In most instances, these monies must be expended within the fiscal year and may not be earmarked for future goals. The end result is that the money is often spent just for the sake of spending it so that the funding will not be terminated in the ensuing year. Useless roads are constructed, useless programs are instituted, all at the taxpayer's expense. It would be far better to hold the money in an interest bearing account until a real need arises. In this way communities could plan for future improvements and services in the areas of their major concerns. There is too much graft and corruption in our present system to allow it to continue.

Any new project, or extension of an existing program, should be carefully researched and a proposal for the expenditure of funds involved submitted to a group of people selected to approve such plans. These individuals should be knowledgeable in community affairs, building construction, existing welfare programs, population trends in their own geographical area, and the whole gamut of local concerns. By virtue of their knowledge and experience, they would be in a position to establish priorities based on need. Any proposed expenditures that they approve should then be put to a vote among the residents of the area involved. No improvements should be made or programs instituted without the sanction of the community as a whole.

A lot of the monies allocated to the states by the federal government must be met with matching funds. These matching funds come out of the individual state's tax revenue without any consideration being given to the actual need for the money that has been granted by the federal government. Consequently, the taxpayers end up paying additional taxes for questionable programs over which they have no control. We must take a stand against such practices and demand an accountability of all expenditures made at the state level. We must insist that our state's annual budget be submitted to the voters for final approval. Deficit spending must cease and any state sales and income tax be curtailed. What cannot be paid for in the current fiscal year must be tabled until such time as the money is availaale. Just as we are expected to live within our means, so must our politicians learn to live with a balanced budget.

At the national level, we must ask for the same kind of accountability that we expect from state and local governments. The federal budget must also be submitted for a vote of approval by the populace. We have every right to know how our tax dollars are being spent. We have a right to veto spending in areas that do not meet with what we consider to be in the best interest of the country. We have a right to veto all expenditures for nuclear research, nuclear armaments, trips to other planets, and aid to foreign countries – unless it is of an emergency nature brought about by a natural disaster. Once we learn to exercise our right to live in a manner that is in keeping with the funds available, we will begin to enjoy a life free of the burden of unnecessary taxation and deprivation. We will no longer be working to support a greed-ridden political system. What we earn will be ours to utilize for our own purposes. As we become masters of our own domain, life will improve in all areas for all of our people. We will once again become a self-sufficient nation. Our pride in our heritage and our accomplishments will be restored.

This is not an impractical daydream, but rather a very realistic approach to solving our present dilemma. In fact, it is the only way that we can continue to exist. Should our government maintain its present rate of spending, it will soon be out of business. It is already on the verge of bankrupcy. The same holds true for many of our major cities. The future does not look very bright.

Once our cities are no longer able to provide for such vital services as police and fire protection, mass transportation, garbage collection, street cleaning, and snow removal, the total disintegration of their society will become almost instantaneous. People will begin to flee the cities, bringing with them the ultimate destruction of the suburban areas that they look to for their salvation. Crime is already rampant on our city streets. Few will venture out after dark for fear of an impending attack by an unknown assailant. This is the case while there is still seemingly adequate police protection. What will happen if it is withdrawn? Without law enforcement, our cities will self-destruct. Without fire protection, every home and business will be a virtual target for pyromaniacs. Without garbage collection, disease will become rampant and rats will be the number one killer. A major earthquake would not be as devastating as the termination of these essential services. From time to time, city workers strike for higher wages. Their limited walkouts give an idea of what it would be like to have permanent layoffs. It is difficult to cope without their services for short periods of time; it would be impossible to cope when there is no end in sight. We cannot, we must not allow this to happen. That is why it is so important for us to have a say as to how our tax dollars are being spent. The future of our cities is far more important than a lot of the programs for foreign aid that the federal government is currently funding. Charity begins at home. We must not jeopardize our own well-being so that we can send arms and ammunition to different parts of the world. Other countries are not our responsibility, our own survival is our prime concern.

We have more freedom in our country than is found in most others. For this we should be very grateful. But what the majority of our people do not have is the means to live as they choose, in the manner they choose, and the ability to enjoy life to the fullest. Many live with sub-standard conditions, unable to do anymore than subsist on a sub-standard diet. Most of our citizens could afford adequate food, clothing, shelter, and recreational activities if they did not have to turn over such a large portion of their earnings to the Internal Revenue Service. What is rightfully ours is being taken from us and there does not seem to be any way to beat the present system. There are so many double and triple taxes that all of our incentive is being diminshed. We work hard to save a little money, only to have to pay tax on the interest we receive for our savings. We have already paid taxes on this money when it was initially earned. Then if we elect to leave any of our savings to our decendants, in the form of an inheritance, it may once again be taxed. We are taxed by the federal government. Many of us are taxed by the state in which we reside. We are taxed by the utility companies for their inefficient management. We are being taxed right out of our ability to survive. We are paying for all the errors of big business. If they have fiscal problems, they just pass the cost on to the consumer. All of this must cease before we find ourselves in a state of bankruptcy.

We have a Social Security program that was enacted into law in 1936 for the purpose of enabling our senior citizens to live out their declining years without being dependent on others for their financial needs. It is funded by taxes paid on the earnings of gainfully employed individuals. Only those who pay into the system, and in some cases their dependents, are eligible for its retirement benefits. It was a well-thought out program and was hailed by many as one of the greatest humanitarian laws of our times. Now, however, the original law has been amended to include an earnings test for people aged sixty-two to seventy, which reduces Social Security benefits by one dollar for each two dollars earned by an individual in excess of an established amount – the current figure is $5,400 a year for those sixty-two to sixty-five, and $7,300 for those over sixty-five. The test penalizes thousands of older people who must continue to work in order to supplement their inadequate incomes, while allowing wealthy retirees with unlimited unearned income to draw their full Social Security benefits. However, once those penalized by the earnings test reach the magic age of seventy, it suddenly becomes legal for them to enjoy the full fruits of their investment in this government plan. Social Security, in itself, does not provide for a very desirable standard of living. In most instances, additional funds are needed if one is to live above the poverty level. It is fine to provide for our senior citizens, but why penalize them if they have the initiative to remain productive in order to better their living conditions. They pay taxes on their earnings. The government is getting a piece of the action and has no right to add to this tax burden by withholding all, or part, of the previously earned Social Security benefits. No other pension plans stipulate that their payments be based on the amount of income earned after retirement.

The land on which we live is a part of our heritage. It belongs to no man but is ours to use as we go through life. Politicians and government officials have no right to decide how it is to be utilized. Farmers should be allowed to cultivate their land and to grow crops that are native to the soil in their geographical area without any restrictions as to the amount produced. At present, the federal government is subsidizing farmers who limit, or curtail, their crop output. The end result is a loss to the consumer who must pay for a rise in food costs, caused by a decrease in the supply. Only an abundance of crops will bring about a decline in the price of farm products.

The same holds true in the manufacture of goods that are necessary in our day-to-day living. Restrictions, in the form of excessive taxation, are placed on the businesses and industries that provide these commodities. This tends to keep production at a level below the consumer's need and thus causes prices to escalate. To cite an example, consider the cost of women's shoes. Production of this essential item has been curtailed to such an extent that the price of a pair of shoes has tripled in recent years. As a result, more and more Americans are buying imported shoes because they cannot afford those made in the United States. Consequently, shoe factories all over the United States have gone out of business by either declaring bankruptcy or just shutting their doors because they could no longer afford to continue their operation. The whole tax structure has prevented them from retaining a sufficient profit margin to increase production, meet their expenses, and set aside some funds for contingencies. For this same reason, private business and industry throughout the country continues to fail. It is a sad state when individuals are deprived of their livelihood because of the greed of their own countrymen. The government has no right to deny those involved in free enterprise the ability to succeed by usurping their profits.

It is becoming more and more apparent that we must take a stand, on our own behalf, to put an end to what is happening in our country. We cannot continue with the status quo. But where do we begin to put a stop to the strong arm of the government that is grasping what is rightfully ours? Physical violence will do no good, although many may be tempted to follow that route. We will be far better off if we resort to peaceful means to bring a halt to the present system of taxation. We can make known our demands for a more equitable means of financing the federal government by flooding the mail to our elected officials, stating the need for a balanced budget to be submitted to the general public for approval. If this is not done before the next presidential election, we should then choose a candidate on the basis of this as his platform. The person selected need not be a member of any political party. Following the election of a leader who promises to live within the guidelines as set down, we should not tolerate any failure on his part to do so. We should simply refuse to pay income taxes beyond ten percent of our earned income. We will tithe to our country as we are asked to tithe to our church or synagogue. Such a measure will force our leaders to cease spending money in areas that we consider unnecessary. If a balanced budget is submitted to the people and additional funds for a specific program are requested, we have a right to accept or reject what is proposed. If we accept it, we can expect to pay for it.

Several years may pass before any inroads are made on the changes that are needed in our government. It took us over two hundred years to arrive at our present state of affairs; things cannot be rectified overnight. We will all have to practice patience and tolerance as we undertake to right the wrongs of the past. There will always be those who will disagree with what we are trying to achieve but they, no doubt, will be individuals who feel the negative effects of our more stringent policies. Do not heed any cries of woe. They will only serve as a deterrent to the success of what must be accomplished. Let those who weep find their own solution to their problems. Should they decide to join forces with the seekers of a more frugal existence, they will find their place in the general scheme of things. We cannot begin to try to appease all who are left without their "golden egg". It is not our responsibility. We must strive to serve the masses; not the self-appointed recipients of the taxpayer's money. Once they realize that their halcyon days are over, they will find other means of survival. It is human nature to do what is necessary to meet one's basic needs. Things may not be to their liking, but they will soon come to realize that what must be done will be done in spite of their hue and cry. Do not be concerned about any repercussions, just carry on in the knowledge that what we are endeavoring to achieve is in the best interest of the majority of the people.

We have given our elected officials enough free reign; given any more, they will only hang all of us. We can no longer live with unfulfilled promises of better days ahead. We must take the "bull by the horns" and lead the way to the restoration of a lifestyle that is in keeping with the premise upon which our country was founded. The right of life, liberty, and the pursuit of happiness for all. The end of government supremacy will be the beginning of government by the people.

Chapter Fourteen

Leadership With Human Concern

Leadership has always played an important role in man's life. In the beginning, there were tribes with tribal leaders who were chosen for their courage and willingness to fight against all obstacles with the good of the tribe foremost in their minds. The tribesmen followed their leader, confident that he alone could aid them in overcoming all adversity. It was a form of hero worship. The death of a leader was a time of great sorrow and also a time of soul-searching to select the best replacement for the lost leader. No one was ever chosen because he asked for the job or offered to barter his possessions for the honor. A successor was chosen because of his own personal qualities of greatness, esteem, and courage.

We have come a long way since these early days but when it comes to leadership, we have not improved our lot. At times, our country has been led by the kind of men necessary to its growth and development but, of late, men of this caliber have not been available to us. We have had to settle for less than second best. Let us take a look at the qualities and dedication of some of the early presidents who helped to shape the course of our history as a nation.

"Father, I cannot tell a lie, I did it with my own little hatchet," was young George Washington's supposed reply when asked who had cut down a newly planted cherry tree. Whether or not this famous story is true, it does very aptly describe those qualities of honesty and integrity that everyone found in the first president of our country.

Among his many attributes, Washington's ability as a scientific farmer is noteworthy. He kept abreast of all the latest European discoveries and was the first large planter in Virginia to rotate his crops, thus breaking away from the ruinous one-crop tobacco system. He also experimented with various combinations of soils, fertilizers, and seeds in order to insure the best crops and to maintain the fertility of the soil.

Washington's role as an American patriot surfaced when he was unanimously elected Commander-in-Chief of the combined armies of the Colonies on June 15, 1775. For Washington, it was the beginning of six long, exhausting years of campaigning. The first encounter between British soldiers and American militia had already taken place at Lexington and Concord. By the end of 1776, New York had been lost, Washington had retreated through the Jerseys, and the morale of the American patriots had reached an all-time low. Then, with a stroke of genius and courage, on Christmas eve 1776, Washington brought new hope to their cause. His plan was to cross the Delaware River by night and surprise the Hessians who were encamped on the other side in Trenton. The crossing was made extremely difficult because of the prevailing weather conditions of snow and ice, but by 4:00 a.m., the army had safely reached the Jersey shore and landed nine miles north of their destination. The march to Trenton was very hazardous as the snow had turned to rain and hail, making the roads treacherous. The surprise attack caught the Hessians totally unprepared. Washington had been right in his judgment that the effects of the Christmas festivities would leave the enemy very vulnerable. His victory was complete with a loss of only four or five men and the capture of over a thousand prisoners. Washington's patience, determination, and unshakeable courage kept his army together until October 19, 1781, when Lord Cornwallis, leader of the British army, surrendered at Yorktown. On December 23, 1783, Washington appeared before Congress and resigned his commission as Commander-in-Chief, but his days of service to his country were not over.

Upon the adoption of the Constitution, the first Presidential Electoral College met in February 1789 to select the country's first president. The unanimous choice was George Washington who had proven himself as both a statesman and a soldier. He went on to serve two terms, providing the new nation with a vigorous administration and the leadership needed to guide it through its first stages of development. He was unwilling to serve any longer.

Thomas Jefferson served as president from 1801 to 1809. He graduated, after two years of study, from William and Mary College in 1762. He then studied law for the next five years and was admitted to the bar in Virginia in 1767. The following year he was elected to the Virginia House of Burgesses. Jefferson was also a self-taught architect and designed his own home, Monticello.

Thomas Jefferson is probably best remembered for his role in drafting the Declaration of Independence. In 1776, the Second Continental Congress still hesitated to make a final break with Britain. A committee of five was appointed, with Thomas Jefferson as chairman, to draw up a formal declaration. Most of the work was done by Jefferson in his lodgings in Philadelphia. He delivered his draft of the Declaration of Independence to Congress on June 28, 1776. It was officially adopted on July 4th of the same year.

His political career was just beginning. In 1779, he was elected Governor of Virginia. He was re-elected to Congress in 1783 and was sent to France to assist John Adams and Benjamin Franklin in their efforts to negotiate commercial treaties with foreign powers. He remained in France for five years serving as Minister for the last three. He returned home in 1789, at which time President Washington appointed him Secretary of State. In 1797, he was elected Vice-President and served as President of the Senate. In this capacity, he prepared a Manual of Parlimentary Practice which has since been the standard by which the proceedings of legislative bodies in this country are governed. In 1800, Jefferson was nominated for and became the third President of the United States. He was re-elected in 1804 for a second term. His architectural interests again surfaced and he undertook the beautification of the President's House and its surrounding landscape.

Abraham Lincoln was born in a log cabin in Hardin County, Kentucky. The little education that he received was the result of his own efforts. He began his upward climb in 1832 when he served as a Captain of Volunteers during the Black Hawk War. He was made postmaster of his home town, New Salem, Illinois, in 1833 and later served as the county surveyor. In 1834, he was elected to the legislature and retained his seat for six years. During this time he also studied law, was admitted to the bar, and began practicing.

Lincoln became involved in national politics in 1856 when he joined the Republican Party. Two years later, he was nominated for senator and ran against Stephen Douglas. Although Douglas won the election, Lincoln gained many supporters by challenging Douglas to a series of debates. They dealt with just one topic – slavery. In 1860, Lincoln was nominated as the Republican candidate for president. When he took his oath of office as the sixteenth President of the United States on March 4, 1861, the preservation of the Union was uppermost in his mind.

On April 12, 1861, Fort Sumter, then in the hands of the Union, was fired upon by Confederate forces. Two days later, Lincoln issued a call for 75,000 militia. The response from every section of the North was overwhelming, as men came to enlist to serve in defense of the Union. During the first year and a half of the Civil War, the question of slavery did not arise. The fight to preserve the Union was the dominant issue. However, it was not long before the forces against slavery began to demand that the government take action. Lincoln sincerely wanted slavery abolished; he felt that it had no place in a country founded on the principles of freedom for all. Still, his paramount duty was to save the Union, with or without slavery.

Lincoln prepared a document concerning slavery which he presented to the Cabinet at a meeting on July 22, 1862. The members approved it but a decision was made to withhold its contents from the public until a major Union victory could be announced. On September 17, 1862, General Lee was defeated an Antietam, Maryland. This victory halted the threatened invasion of the North and sent the Confederate forces into retreat. It also paved the way for Lincoln to issue his great proclamation: that all persons held as slaves within the states, or designated parts of states, in rebellion against the government on the first of January 1863, should be free.

Lincoln took the oath of office for the second time on March 4, 1865. The war was drawing to a close and he was busy with his plans for reconstruction. The surrender of General Lee on April 9, 1865 brought immense relief to the President. On the night of April 14th, 1865, Lincoln accompanied his wife and two friends to the Ford Theatre, there he was shot and mortally wounded by John Wilkes Booth.

"Intellectual supremacy is good, physical prowess desirable, but better than all, and without which none can succeed, is an upright character." These were the words of Theodore Roosevelt as he spoke to the students of Northwestern University in Evanston, Illinois shortly after he had taken the oath of office as the 26th President. Roosevelt graduated from Harvard University and studied law at Columbia University before becoming interested in politics. His political career began in 1881 when he was elected to the New York legislature. In 1889, President Harrison appointed him civil service commissioner. He served in this capacity until 1895, resigning to become president of the Police Board of New York City. In 1897, he was called back to Washington to serve as Assistant Secretary of the Navy under President McKinley.

When war with Spain was declared in 1898, Roosevelt was appointed lieutenant colonel of a cavalry unit. He drilled and trained with the regiment in Texas before being ordered to Cuba. He was successful in leading his Rough Riders to victory on San Juan Hill as he rode among them and urged them on.

In the fall of 1898, Roosevelt was elected Governor of New York State. This was followed, two years later, by his being elected Vice President of the United States. On the day of President McKinley's death, by assassination, September 14, 1901, Roosevelt took the oath of office as President. He was later nominated for President by the Republican Party in 1904 and won the election by a large majority. One of the highlights of his administration was his bringing about a meeting between Russia and Japan for a Peace

Conference, which was held at Portsmith, New Hampshire. These two countries had been at war for two years and ending the war was the primary interest of the whole world. Roosevelt was highly praised for his efforts and in 1906 was awarded the Nobel prize for services in the interest of peace.

One of the most notable achievements of Roosevelt's career was the purchase of the Isthmus of Panama in 1904 for the purpose of constructing an inter-oceanic canal. The work was begun during his administration in 1906 and the great canal was completed in 1914.

There must be men in our country today with the ability to successfully lead us in our present struggle for survival. However, we have fallen into a state of lethargy when it comes to electing public officials. We do not demand true leadership but accept any candidates offered even though we are aware of all of their shortcomings. When given a choice between two ineffectual contestants, we often choose to make no decision and refrain from casting our vote. This does not help the situation as it in no way indicates our dissatisfaction with those selected to run for office. It would be far better to write in the name of a person we consider suitable for the position as a way to indicate our disapproval. It is possible to change the established method of selecting public officials but it will take initiative and a great deal of concentrated effort by a vast majority of our countrymen to bring about such a change. If enough people are discontent with the existing situation, it will not be difficult to enlist their support in an effort to put an end to the status quo and to begin to seek out men and women who have the qualities necessary to lead our country with honesty and dignity.

Somewhere in this land there must be a person who is deserving of being chosen for this honor by virtue of his integrity and moral desire to contribute to the good will of the country and all of its populace. He need not be wealthy or from an old established family; nor should age, sex, or national origin be a factor. However, by virtue of our Constitution, he must be a natural-born citizen and be over thirty-five years of age. Who do you know among your associates who might fit the bill? Who do you know who has led an exemplary life; has the ability to overcome obstacles without resorting to violence; has set an example for others to follow in his dealings with his fellow man; is capable of making decisions based on the greatest good for the greatest number; has a feeling for all God's creatures and a desire to preserve the environment in its natural state; is willing to put the good of the country before personal gain; will work to improve the plight of the disadvantaged, the infirmed, the aged; will endeavor to terminate the technological advances and nuclear experiments that are causing so many problems in our lives; and will put an end to the possibility of our country's use of nuclear warfare for all time? We must look for an individual who does not adhere to the dogma of any particular religion, but who has an understanding of the need for all to follow their own innate desire for a way of life that suits their philosophy and cultural customs. Our country has been termed a "melting pot", as it is a conglomerate of many different nationalities and religious preferences. There is no one way that will be acceptable to all of our people. Patience and tolerance of one's fellow man are essential characteristics of anyone we choose as our leader.

From time to time we hear about the heroic attempts of certain individuals to perform a great service for their country or countrymen. We honor these people for their efforts, not because they seek recognition, but because of their willingness to give of themselves to benefit others. Their goal is not to gain self-esteem or power, but rather to improve conditions for mankind. These are the kind of people that we should look to for leadership. It is the lack of this type of personality at the helm that is causing a great deal of our present day problems. We are being governed by men who are only serving their own interests and special interest groups and are not concerned with what is best for the country. They may profess great love for the common man, but their actions reveal that their real intent is to gain power, adulation, and monetary wealth for themselves. We must seek leaders who are not of this self-serving nature. Money should not be the key to opening the door to public office. As long as the major political "plums" are for sale to the highest bidder, we will not have public officials who are dedicated to bringing peace and harmony to our nation. These offices must be earned, not bought, if we are to be governed by politicians whom we can respect.

It is time for a change in the whole structure of our political system. We must begin to hold public officials accountable for their actions and expenses. They should be made to keep a record, subject to an annual audit, of all expenditures charged to the taxpayers. At present our tax dollars are being used to pay for the luxurious living enjoyed by those in high public office. This is a very serious mistake as it is depriving the masses of the right to use their wages for their own personal expenses. Elected government personnel should receive an adequate salary, with no fringe benefits other than an annual vacation, sick leave, health insurance, and retirement benefits. Any traveling that they choose to do must be done on their own time and at their own expense. This, of course, does not apply to the president, or the person designated to act on his behalf. The head of state must be free to travel as necessary and to receive the frills and special privileges that are in keeping with the dignity of his position. Adequate security must be provided during his term of office and the White House, as we have come to know the official residence of the president, should be maintained for the use of the first family.

It is quite obvious that unless we have a change in the manner in which our country is being led, we are all going to be in a state of dire need. We cannot afford to live with the misuse of funds that now exists. The greed of our politicians must not be allowed to flourish. This can only be done by a change in the policies of our government. Those now in authority are not going to do much more than continue "to feather their own nests".

It will, no doubt, be easier to start at the local level to initiate changes and to seek out the kind of leadership needed to put an end to the present "reign of terror". As you go about your daily chores, try to think of a person, in your geographical area, that you would like to see in a position of political responsibility; a person whom you feel has the human concerns of his fellow man foremost in his mind. Talk to your friends and relatives about drafting such an individual for an office of importance in your community. Invite the person of your choice to meet with small groups of people, so that he can learn of their concerns and make his own beliefs known. A pot of coffee is not much to invest in improving conditions for yourself and your neighbors. If you do not meet with success in having your candidate's name on the ballot at election time, you will have to resort to the use of a write-in vote.

There is no need to ever vote for a candidate who does not have the qualifications necessary to do the job.

As we enlist new people for public office in our own communities, we can gradually groom them for positions at the state level. It will be a stepping-stone process to move people who prove their worth onto positions of more responsibility. Our ultimate goal will be to make an impact at the national level but we must be careful not to attract a great deal of attention to ourselves. This must be a quiet endeavor that simmers below the surface and does not reach its full impetus until the day of reckoning arrives. There are too many lobbyists on the national scene who will go to any extreme to champion their own cause. These are the people we must avoid and who must not be aware of the challenge we are going to present.

Big business is the backbone of today's political process. The decision as to who will be the next president is made behind closed doors. This person is selected by those who are in positions of wealth, power and authority. The will of the people is never a consideration. The stakes are much higher. There is no way that the average citizen can come out ahead with the present system. Great cuts in spending are advocated but not in areas that will benefit the masses. There are ways to cut expenses. There are ways to bring our country back to a sound economy, but it is not the way that is now being advocated by those who seek advances in technology, nuclear armaments, defense spending, space travel, and foreign aid, with little or no regard for the well-being of the common man.

The next election can be an exciting time as we begin to make inroads in changing the political process in our own communities. It will be the first step in initiating reforms at all levels of government. If we start today, we can be well on our way by the time of the next presidential election to overcoming the present method of selecting our head of state. We can, instead, bring about the election of a leader who is beholden to no party, political platform, or campaign promises. There is a way to provide leadership with human concern for our sinking ship. The lifeline is in our hands.

A national moratorium may very well decide our next presidential election.

Chapter Fifteen
The Will Of The People Shall Prevail

We have always put our political leaders on a pedestal and looked up to them, trusting that they would do what was best for the country. Lately, we have become disillusioned and have come to the realization that they are as subject to human failings as the rest of humanity. They may mean no harm but because of their lack of sound judgment, they make errors and cause problems that might have been averted. "To err is human, to forgive divine", but when the country as a whole must suffer the consequences of political mistakes, forgiveness is not so easy to live with. It would be far better to try to eliminate the possibility of such blunders and to save our forgiveness for mistakes made in areas that will not lead us into a national catastrophe.

The primary issues that elected officials of the federal government are presently charged with resolving are, in general: national defense, foreign affairs, the federal budget, and domestic problems. The latter includes: health, education, welfare, energy, unemployment, inflation, recession, social security, and environmental concerns. Now we all know that we want to put an end to defense spending; to conserve energy; to have a balanced national budget; to put an end to unemployment; to conserve our natural resources; to preserve the environment; and to provide for the needs of our people in the areas of food, clothing, shelter, education, medical assistance, and retirement benefits. With these decisions already determined, our politicians should be able to set their goals and objectives with very little difficulty. Every political office should have a written job description that spells out the duties it entails. Those running for office will then have no need to travel throughout the fifty states telling us what they are going to do if elected. The acceptance of a public office should carry with it the responsibility to fulfill the obligations it imposes. Once such guidelines have become an established practice, we will cease to be at the mercy of our elected officials. They will no longer be empowered to spend tax dollars in areas that are not within their concern; nor will they be in a position to "line their own pockets". Those who do not live up to what they have agreed to, as part of their platform for election, should be removed from office. This may seem like a cruel and unnecessary measure; however, we do not retain employees in the business world whose job performance is not satisfactory. All must undergo periodic performance evaluations by their superiors, and an unsatisfactory review that is not rectified leads to termination of the employee's position. Elected officials should be subject to this same kind of appraisal. A committee of men knowledgeable in the affairs of state should be appointed by the president to evaluate the job performance of those who hold office on Capitol Hill.

Members of the Senate and House of Representatives should be required to attend all sessions, to arrive promptly, and to stay until the session ends. Consideration should, of course, be given for extenuating circumstances. Those who do not comply with the existing rules and regulations should be removed from office. Our Constitution has made provision for filling such vacancies:

> *Article XVII: When vacancies happen in the representation of any State in the Senate, the executive authority of such State shall issue writs of election to fill such vacancies: provided, that the legislature of any State may empower the executive thereof to make temporary appointments until the people fill the vacancies by election as the legislature may direct.*

The greatest good for the greatest number must always prevail, therefore, one man's transgressions cannot go unheeded.

Thomas Jefferson called a legislative tyranny the worst of all tyrannies. James Madison, in presenting his Bill of Rights to Congress in 1789, said the guarantees of liberty must be leveled chiefly "against the legislative for it is the most powerful, and the most likely to be abused, because it is under the least control." It was for this reason that the framers of the Constitution endowed the representatives with the power of impeachment and the senators the power to try those accused.

> *Article II, section 4 of the Constitution: The President, Vice President, and all civil officers of the United States, shall be removed from office on Impeachment for, and Conviction of, Treason, Bribery, or other High Crimes and Misdemeanors.*

Civil officers do not include military officers nor legislatures. The latter are not considered officers in the constitutional sense. Why should any of our politicians who are deficient in their work performance, or who are dishonest with their constituents, be exempt from this same type of reprimand?

Military personnel who do not serve their country with honor are disciplined in accordance with the articles contained in the Military Code of Justice. Provisions are made, under Article 15, for non-judicial punishment of minor infractions without resorting to the criminal court process. It is a slap-on-the-wrist kind of punishment that does not go on record as a federal conviction. More serious breaches of military law are dealt with by court martial: a court consisting of military personnel for the trial of offenses against military law. There are three types of courts: summary, special, and general. The latter handles the most serious offenses and is the one that can hand down a dishonorable discharge.

Congressmen do not need a monumental staff in order to carry out their duties. Most of the people they employ are there solely to promote the public image and to insure the re-election of their employer. Countless hours are spent on mailings to constituents who probably never bother to read what is sent to them. There is only one criterion for being re-elected and that is a satisfactory job performance. The allocation of staff should be the same for all members of Congress; one is no more deserving than another. Those who truly want to serve their country will do so without all the frills that have become expected as "perks" of the job.

If ours is to be a "government of the people, by the people, and for the people" (Abraham Lincoln in his Gettysburg Address, November 1863), then so let it be! The majority must rule and take an active part in what is going on in Washington. Professional lobbying must be eliminated as a means of influence. Our elected officials must be mandated to carry out the will of the people they serve. As long as we sit idly by and permit politicians to do their own bidding, we will suffer the effects of their incompetence. This is not to say that all of our elected officials are not doing a good job, however, there are enough who are deficient in their performance to warrant our concern. Once they are aware of the fact that they must abide by the wishes of those who have elected them to office, that they have a responsibility to their constituents and are answerable to no others, they will have a better understanding of their role and their reason for being in a leadership position. Acceptance of this premise will make their job easier. It will merely be a matter of keeping in touch with home base with regard to questions that are coming up for consideration. By seeking advice and information from those who will be involved and affected by the results of the decisions made on Capitol Hill, our representatives will have the input needed to cast their vote in keeping with the desires of their constituents. Many issues that are decided at the national level should be decided at the local level as this is their area of concern. Who in Washington can tell us how to run our local school system; who can decide what should be done about unemployment in our geographical area? Only those who live with these problems on a daily basis are in a position to make sound judgments on such matters. The consensus of the majority is needed in order to make intelligent political decisions; no one resident of an area, even if he is an elected representative, should be in a position to have the final say on any issue. This holds true at all levels of government. Matters of concern to the individual states must be brought to the attention of those who reside within their territorial boundaries. Opinion polls, in the form of mailed questionnaires, should be taken regarding any new action that is up for consideration. People will respond as long as they know that their advice will be heeded. Input from the general public must be an ongoing process.

There is little doubt that the will of the people will eventually be made known and brought to a state of fulfillment. The question is what form will such action take? If our political community as a whole does not acquiesce to the demands of the masses and go with the flow of the tide, then force will in all probability be the next step. We are not going to sit back and watch our country self-destruct without asserting ourselves. Therefore, it is important that our elected officials heed the voice of the people and take measures to remedy existing conditions. The gravy train can no longer run for the chosen few, we must all travel together with a common destination – the equality of all men to share in the management of the affairs of their country.

In order to keep abreast of what is happening on the political scene and to take an active role in the decision making process of government, you might want to consider forming a discussion group in your neighborhood (a neighborhood can be a city block or a rural township) to weigh the pros and cons of forthcoming legislative actions. This will enable you to become familiar with the thinking of others who, because of their individual situations, may see things in a different light. A monthly newsletter from your representatives would be a useful tool in keeping your discussions relevant. The date for such mailings could be used to determine the time for your meetings, thus insuring your having the latest issues to discuss. Not everyone will want to be involved in this type of activity, however, if each family would send one representative to relay their thinking and bring back news and pertinent information, the desired purpose could be accomplished.

We all know how we would like to live and for the most part we should be able to achieve what we consider to be the ideal state. This will be different for each individual, still most will agree on the need for adequate food, clothing, shelter, and recreation. Just how we translate these requirements into our own lifestyle will be reflected by our unique personalities. Nevertheless, these are the basic needs that we must keep in mind as we go about initiating changes in our present system of government. The common good of all of our countrymen must be our ultimate goal. This is our only responsibility. As you are being asked to consider a variety of different issues, you need only reflect on what their acceptance will be in these terms. Gradually you can expand your concerns to include problem-solving in the areas of: education, medical assistance, food stamps, welfare payments, unemployment compensation, preservation of our natural resources, protection of all wildlife, the condition of the environment, and whatever else might come to the fore that will improve the quality of our lives. Once a plan of action has been set up for dealing with these issues, we will have an idea of how to proceed and the whole endeavor will seem a lot less complicated and a lot less mind-boggling. With all of our "ducks in order," there will be no need to alter our course; what is right for us will be right for ensuing generations. As Robert Frost, the renowned English poet of the twentieth century, said, "Most of the change that we see in life is just truth being in and out of favor."

At times, we may be apt to feel that we are powerless in the face of all the adversity that besets us. We may be ready to acquiesce to those who foresee the end of all that is without even putting up a struggle. Why bother? What good can we do? No one will ever listen to us. Others have tried but to no avail. This, of course, is a very pessimistic attitude and one that is not in keeping with our heritage. We fought for our rights in the past and were successful, we can do so again. Actually, it may not even be very difficult. Those who are now in office are floundering. They do not admit to this, yet they are well aware that they are grasping at straws in order to bring some semblance of sanity to the chaotic mess in which they find themselves. Unable to solve one problem, they move on to another, hoping to have some small success with which to appease the people, but success is not forthcoming. There is dissension in the ranks. Of course, those at the helm are putting up a bold and courageous front. The show must go on! However, there is no director to call a halt to the scene as it is now being played. There is no one to rewrite the script that is currently being enacted. By now any voice out of the wilderness would be considered a blessing. A demand on the part of the citizens of the country to be given a chance to exercise their rights would, undoubtedly, be considered a welcome request by those who are in power. They may not acknowledge these sentiments, however, they would not be likely to offer any opposition to such a proposal. The people would become masters of their own fate and any gross errors made in the affairs of the government would be of their doing. The present regime would no longer be responsible for the future of this nation.

Now how do we begin to assert ourselves and make our voices heard? Once we have organized into small neighborhood groups, we should make a list of all the things that need to be done to improve the quality of life in the area of our concern. We should send a copy of this list to our elected representatives and ask them to vote affirmatively on any action up for consideration that will better the conditions as listed. Then, to broaden our horizons, we should call a joint meeting of all the neighborhood groups within our communities and invite our representatives to meet with these people so that all can hear what they have to say in response to the action that is being proposed. We should also inform them that our vote for their re-election will be contingent upon their compliance with our request. Very few will "bite the hand that feeds them". Our politicians want to keep their jobs and they will if they learn to play the game by the rules as set down, to bring the greatest good to the greatest number in the area that they represent. They may even be grateful to have a legitimate excuse to vote against issues that they are being pressured to support.

The will of the people must prevail. The future of this nation and our very survival must be put into our own hands. We must unite behind a common goal and refuse to sanction any ego trips our politicians decide to embark on so that we can once again be in control of our destiny. It is up to each and everyone of us to play an active role, in some small way, in the continued effort to keep our country on the road to eventual peaceful and purposeful pursuits for all of its people.

Chapter Sixteen
The Prophets Told Us "How"

Time and again man has tried to circumvent the teachings of the ancient prophets and to take command of his own life without any thought as to what is right or what is wrong. This has been the cause of a majority of the problems that have beset the human race. We cannot ignore the teachings of the Ten Commandments and expect to live with peace and happiness. These words were never intended to be taken lightly. It will only be by reasserting our desire to abide by what has been written, as a guide to living, that we will come to know the true meaning of life. These are not difficult lessons to follow. They are just basic, simple truths that were meant for all men throughout all ages; not just for some men at some time in history. These teachings are not based on race, creed, color, or sex. What is right for one man is right for all.

We would, no doubt, fare better if we were to start today to live in accord with what was set down for us so long ago. It certainly will do no harm to give it a try. Granted, we are all free agents, but not so free as to be able to circumvent these instructions for living with decency and honor, and still come out ahead. The Ten Commandments are recorded in the Old Testament in the Book of Deuteronomy. For those who are not familiar with Biblical history; they were given to Moses as he led his people out of Egypt in search of the Promised Land. They were to guide them as they journeyed on their way. Simply stated in today's language, the Ten Commandments tell us that we must not worship false gods; nor should we sanction the actions of those who do. We must practice moderation in all areas of our lives. We must show respect for our parents, which in present day terms would also include those persons in a position of authority. We must not kill our fellow man. We must not lie, steal, or commit adultery. We must rid ourselves of all forms of greed. We must not discount these teachings for they are the way for all men to live with peace and joy for all time.

Now it is quite obvious that we have been ignoring these words of wisdom. We worship money and honor those who meet with the greatest success in the acquisition of material goods. We live with excesses in all areas of our lives. Respect for law and order is a thing of the past. Murder is on the upswing; stealing is a way of life for many. Honesty is a quality that is no longer held in esteem; lying and cheating are the accepted way of dealing with one's fellow man. Our moral standards have deteriorated into a state of virtual non-existence. Greed has brought us to the point of no return as we exhaust our natural resources to fill our drawers, closets, and shelves with things we do not need and cannot use. We are convinced that our way is right, that it is superior in all respects, and that the teachings of those who preceded us on this Earth are of little or no value. We neglect to take into consideration the fact that we are all just human beings. We are no better, smarter, or more cognizant of man's needs than those who came before us and those who will come after us. Man has always struggled to survive, but we are over-extending ourselves in our efforts to do so and the world is not a better place because of us. In the final analysis, we have accomplished nothing of value. The only lesson that we may learn is the error of our ways. Hopefully, future generations will not repeat our mistakes.

We are now in a state of being in which we have little or no faith in our own ability to conquer the problems that confront us. The threat of a nuclear war, inflation, and shortages of essential resources seem to be beyond our power to overcome. There must be someone somewhere who will show us the way out of this dilemma. Because of our anxiety and apprehension, we must be very careful not to be caught up in following a false prophet with evil intent who offers us solutions to all of our problems. It is very easy to be misled and once one embarks on the wrong course, it is very difficult to retreat. We have had examples of this in our time: Hare Krishna, Synanon, the Unification Church, the Church of Scientology, The Children of God, and the People's Temple. We are all well aware of the disastrous end that befell the followers of the latter cult movement.

An event occurred in November of 1978 that shocked the world and put an end to the lives of the nine hundred followers of Jim Jones. The Guyana Massacre, as it came to be known, marked the end of the People's Temple, a church founded and led by the Reverend Jones. Jim Jones began his ministry in 1953, as a pastor of a Methodist Church in Indianapolis. His first parishes were noted for thier fund-raising activities; he was a hustler who knew how to "feather his own nest". Jones later began to practice demagoguery and healing by faith. He was successful in capitalizing on social discontent, however, his healing was a farce. Few people realized that he hired others to perform his "miracles", which were pure medicine show hokum. As Jones "called forth"a a cancerous tumor from a parishioner's body, his assistant would reach his handkerchief-covered hand into the person's throat and dislodge a bloody tumor – a piece of raw meat or chicken entrails that had previously been concealed in the handkerchief.

In 1965, Jones and his followers migrated to California to set up shop. Now he became a "self-proclaimed messiah" and gave his followers the impression that he was omniscient. He hypnotized his flock with his oratorical prowess, demanding their unyielding loyalty and adoration. On the surface he appealed to the poor, the blacks, and the troubled; thus managing to gain endorsement from important public officials. But behind the locked temple doors, he exerted a diabolic power over his people and forced them to fulfill his excessive needs for financial, egotistical, and sexual gratification. Exhibiting traits of megalomania and paranoia, Jones gradually slipped further and further into a state bordering on insanity. When journalists started to expose the brutality, theft, and sexual aberrations in his temple, he fled with his fanatic followers to the jungle of Guyana and organized a tropical socialist commune that turned into a fear-ridden concentration camp. Here he continued to use his spellbinding rhetorical powers to convince the members of the cult that they would always be harassed, persecuted, and driven from their temple, that the only way to achieve true happiness would be by following their leader in a mass suicide. "Everyone has to die," said Jones. "If you love me as much as I love you, we must all die together or be destroyed from the outside." Then he ordered a vat of strawberry Flavour-Aide, laced with tranquilizers and cyanide, brought forth. Many willingly walked up to the battered tub and took their cup of Flavour-Aide; those who were reluctant had the poison poured down their throats. The carnage in Guyana is reminiscent of the Zealots of Masada who killed each other rather than surrender to the Romans in 73 A.D., or of the one thousand Japanese civilians who hurled themselves from a cliff in Saipan as American troops took control of the island during World War II. However, in this instance, it was not a fear of the horrors of war that led to self-slaughter, but rather the paranoia of one individual.

There will always be people who will rise up to preach about the salvation of mankind. Many will stir up large numbers who will willingly become followers of their doctrine. Some are harmless and offer hope of a better way of life; others, as we have seen, are destructive and lead their flocks to doom. Whole countries have been mesmerized by the personality of such a leader, only to realize, too late, the trap into which they had fallen. The question then is, "to whom does one listen"? There must be some criteria by which to judge these self-appointed disciples. Actually, they do not differ very much from those who enter into the ministry. We have good and evil preachers in our churches just as we find good and evil people in all walks of life. How are you to know which of these crusaders are of honorable intent? There are certain signs to look for. Anyone who professes to have God-given powers, to have powers beyond the normal, to have the ability to perform miracles, or who offers salvation if one joins the cult, is to be avoided. A good teacher will not try to make others subservient to his ways through force, threats, or false promises. He will, instead, preach the word of God as it has been written by the true prophets of Biblical times and try to instill the value of living in accord with the Ten Commandments. He may feel inspired to deliver God's message but he will not profess to be a god or lay claim to supernatural powers. To follow such a minister of the gospel will do no harm and it will unite people behind a common cause for good.

We can no longer ignore the only way available to us to once again make our lives worth living. We must begin with ourselves and make a commitment to abide by the principles that have been set down by those who were chosen to deliver the word of the Creator of this planet we call Earth. It will be an individual commitment, that no one can make for us, to ten steps that will lead us back on the path of human dignity. We have strayed too far, however, it will not be difficult to return to a way of life that will put an end to all of our present misery. The small sacrifice we may think we have to make may actually be no sacrifice at all. We punish our children if they do not abide by our wishes. We do not tolerate any disobedience on their part but we do reward them for their good behavior. We have not been asked to do much more than we ask of our children and we, too, can expect to reap the rewards available for complying with the standard of behavior that has been given to us to follow. Once we start to enjoy these new-found benefits, we will never again want to deviate from this path. Those who choose to go in a different direction will never know much more than grief and misery. What we make of our future is up to us. We can be the victims of our own stupidity or we can come out victorious. So, as you reach the end of your rope and have no where else to turn, why not do a complete about face and start anew and accept the premise as set forth at the beginning of civilization. Let each of us begin to acknowledge the presence of a Supreme Being as the guiding force in our lives. Then, let us start to show respect for law and order as a way of establishing a peaceful existence for all. Let us try to develop our own honesty and integrity in our dealings with our fellow man. Let us try to re-establish a moral code for living with a set of values that will bring stability into our homes. Let us foresake our materialistic pursuits and put love of each other above love of our possessions. Let us, in essence, accept the Ten Commandments as our guide for living.

"Ask and ye shall receive" is another part of our spiritual heritage that we have not been taking very seriously. Few of us have given ourselves an opportunity to be the beneficiaries of such great wisdom. It sounds too easy, too good to be true and we do not trust what we do not acquire by our own resourcefulness. Only little children believe they have a right to be the recipients of all that they desire. It does not matter to them how this is achieved; they may make their requests to their parents, God, Santa Claus, or the Good Fairy. In their simple way, they have the answer that would ease the way for all of us to live our lives to the fullest. However, they are all too soon taught, by disbelieving adults, not to be so foolhardy; that life is not a "bowl of cherries", but rather "a school of hard knocks". Gradually, they give up or lose their belief in their divine right to have all their requests granted. They cease to ask for what they want and, therefore, no longer receive what is available to them for the asking. Thus another generation of skeptics forsake their gift of a life of abundance.

There is a way for all of us to tap unseen resources that will aid us in living with the least amount of discord. We need only take the time to sit quietly and wait for answers to come that will show us the way to solve all of our problems. This takes some practice, but it is not difficult. It merely requires clearing the mind of all thoughts, so as to allow for the free flow of ideas. The answers that you seek may come almost instantly or it may take several attempts on your part before you begin to receive mental impressions. There will be nothing startling or unusual as you proceed, it will just be as if you were picking up ideas in your mind. They will come in the form of a thought as to what is right for you to do in a given situation. You probably will have been dwelling on the problem prior to your seeking a solution so there will be no need to concentrate on it any further. The response that you receive may be different from what you anticipated but it will feel right and you will be comfortable with the proposed course of action. This practice is known in many cultures as "meditating" and has been used as a method of dealing with life situations for as far back as man is able to trace his beginning. Primitive man was always in touch with his "spirit-guide" and sought his advice on all major changes under consideration by the tribe. If this practice worked then, there is no reason why it will not work now. If it works for others, there is no reason why it will not work for you. However, a certain amount of trust is necessary in this type of discipline because when you act on the answers received, you do not initially know if they are going to bring about the desired results. As you meet with success in these endeavors, you will gradually develop confidence in your ability. It will become a part of your daily experience and be a source of information that you will not want to relinquish. Should you experience a strong negative feeling when you contemplate a particular action, it would be wise to heed such feelings as what you are about to do may not be right for you or in your own best interest.

The road ahead is going to be difficult enough without our trying to go it alone. We need all the help that we can muster to ease the way. There is no need to flounder, to rely solely on our own judgment, or the advice of well-meaning friends. We need only open our minds to those untapped resources that will provide answers to all of life's challenges, help us to overcome all obstacles, and allow us to live free from fear of making a mistake in any area of concern. We need only follow the advice that has been given to us as the way to conduct our lives.

The animal kingdom lives by its own set of rules. They seem to fare better than we do as a result of a respect for an instinctive code of behavior and a sensitivity to their inner feelings that guide them in coping with the elements with which they must live.

We are not alone as we make our way in this world. We are watched over and protected but we can refuse to be the recipients of these God-given gifts. The choice is ours. We may accept or reject what is available to us for the asking. We can live in fear of the future or we can cast all our burdens aside and enjoy life, secure in the knowledge that All Will Be Well.

Chapter Seventeen
A Return To The Good Old Ways

At the beginning of time, man had to fend for himself and be responsible for his own survival. Rarely was there another person to aid him in his tasks. Each individual realized that he must seek food and shelter in order to maintain himself. Young were cared for but only until they were able to deal with the elements and their environment in a responsible manner; they were not pampered and coddled. Basically, life was a matter of "every man for himself". Gradually, family units began to develop and interpersonal relationships entered the picture. Now a whole new dimension was added to man's existence; human nature had to be dealt with; sharing had to be learned, understood, and accepted. Life became a bit more complicated but it was also more enjoyable. With shared responsibilities, there was more time to devote to activities that were not totally of a survival nature. Thus we had the beginning of what we now term leisure time.

We have come a long way since these early days in our methods of providing for our basic needs and have developed some very scientific approaches to interpersonal relationships. Life is certainly more comfortable. Food, clothing, and shelter are available without any thought as to their origin. They are taken for granted as our inalienable right to possess, to be supplied with, and to enjoy. Now we are concerned with supplying those other "things" that we deem necessary to our well-being. We have embarked on a lifestyle of total self-indulgence in the area of materialistic pursuits and self-gratification; we consider our ways to be so superior to those of our forebearers. But are they? Medical research teams are now being challenged to find cures for the diseases created as a result of our ever-increasing pollution of the air, the water, and the food we eat. We have advanced our technology beyond our need for such sophisticated knowledge and are frightened, confused, and at a loss as to what to do in order to right the wrongs of our over-zealous pursuits. We are confronted with the problems of alcoholism, drug abuse, crime and violence in all walks of life. Certainly, we had every right to improve conditions in order to make our lives more pleasurable than what was experienced by primitive man, but we do not have the right to make this planet uninhabitable for future generations. Rather, we owe it to them to return it to a state that is in keeping with its original purpose of providing man with his basic needs for survival.

Many of us are inclined to think that the world situation will improve if we can just wait a little longer, that the pendulum will soon begin to swing the other way. We have always been confronted with broad ranges of behavior and attitudes. We moved from the Victorian Age to the Roaring Twenties and then back again to the more conservative Fifties. Therefore, with time, things should start to fall in place as a new conservatism overtakes our country. This, however, is just wishful thinking on our parts. We have gone too far off course for such an easy solution. Things are not going to improve without a conscientious effort on our part to change our individual lifestyles. In essence, the pendulum has been broken by our own greed. It is not just a minor crack that can be repaired but a major break that calls for a complete replacement of all parts before it can be of any further use in changing the course of events.

History is known to repeat itself and it would be to our advantage to start now to emulate some of the ways of those who lived in previous times. Not the era we read about of Victorian prudishness, but somewhere in between then and now, there must be a happy medium that would allow us to live free from the overly conservative behavior of our predecessors and the excessively premissive attitudes of the present day. A time when our ancestors were content with less, depending more on the land for their survival, and did not pursue great technological advances; when they lived by their own ability to hunt, fish, and cultivate the land and were satisfied as long as they had adequate food, clothing, shelter, and friends and loved ones with whom they could share their leisure time. Their houses, for the most part, were small but adequate. They did not enjoy our modern conveniences of running water, central heating, air conditioning, inside plumbing, or all the modern appliances we now rely upon to ease the burden of our daily chores. Still they were content with their lifestyle, their days were filled with activity, and they had little time to dream of being carried away to some far-off land where riches abound. They were not obsessed with the pursuit of material goods but enjoyed what was available to them and did not try to outdo each other in their acquisition of monetary wealth. Life was lived on a day-to-day basis, tomorrow would be dealt with in the sequence of time. Families were generally self-sustaining units and relied very little on others to supply them with the means of survival. They were independent people, willing to help others when necessary, yet were mainly concerned with their own well-being.

We may pride ourselves on the advances we have made in the fields of medicine, technology, and humanitarian projects, yet are we any better able to enjoy our lives than those who came before us? We may travel farther and faster, have more creature comforts, and know that the Moon is not populated by other living beings; nevertheless, we pay for these great strides forward with stress, pollution, shortages of natural resources, and the threat of an all-out nuclear war. All of these giant steps forward are only putting us in a position to begin to take a few steps backward; to stop somewhere in between "where we are" and where we were". We will be better, happier people when we come to terms with the reality of our situation and the course of action we must follow in order to survive in the years to come. We need not give up all of our modern appliances, they are an asset in our lives and serve a useful purpose. What we might consider giving up, instead, is our utilization of vast amounts of synthetic products made from petroleum. Petroleum comes from the earth as a dark liquid that contains hundreds of different liquids which are the raw materials for making thousands of other products. It is changed chemically to make:

Ethylene: from which food containers, garden hoses, phonograph records, and anti-freeze are made.
Acetylene: from which plastics and adhesives are made.
Propylene: from which explosives and laundry detergents are made.
Butylene: from which rubber is made.
Tolvene: from which TNT is made.
Xlene: from which paints and Dacron are made.

Other by-products of petroleum are anesthetics, antiseptics, chewing gum, cleaning fluid, cosmetics, fertilizers, furniture polish, glue, laundry sizing, medicines, parafin wax, petroleum jelly, printer's ink, wax paper, nylon, rayon, asphalt, gasoline, L.P. gas, kerosene, crude oil, diesel oil, fuel oil, jet fuel, and lubricating oil. Before we become involved in a global war over a shortage of these commodities, we would be wise to take stock of our own use of the by-products of petroleum and find other ways to achieve the same results. Our ancestors got along very nicely without most of these artificially created substances.

In the "good old days", produce was not shipped back and forth across the country; each geographical area took care of its own needs. Home canning and preserving ensured everyone enough to eat all year round. Specialty items were purchased at the local store, but most foodstuffs were home grown, home canned, home baked, and prepared from "scratch". Today we rely a great deal on frozen foods, packaged goods, and fruits and vegetables that are transported from the west to the east and the south to the north. We are no longer self-sufficient in our own communities and this is not to our credit. Actually, foods that are consumed in the region in which they are grown are far more nutritious than those that are shipped great distances under questionable conditions. Transportation also adds to the final purchase price which ultimately includes the cost of handling, packaging, shipping, as well as the salaries of those involved in the total process. We would fare better if we were to revert back to those bygone days and re-establish our own local supply of the foods necessary to meet the nutritional needs of the people who reside in the area. We may have to resort to solar heat as a means of providing year round produce, but it is not an impossible feat. Just as greenhouses are able to supply us with flowers on a continuing basis, they should also be able to provide us with fruits and vegetables. If we can send men to the Moon, we should be capable of growing fresh produce in the winter months. We would certainly be most grateful for our ability to sustain ourselves if we were to suddenly become the victims of a natural disaster, a nationwide transportation strike, or an attack on our country by the armed forces of another nation. We have become rather complacent in our attitude toward the possibility of such an assault, but that does not guarantee our immunity.

To better understand the manner in which the early settlers of our country lived, you might want to plan to visit a restored area of historical significance. Williamsburg, Virginia is an excellent example of the simplicity of the lifestyle of past generations. This quiet, slow, and remarkably unpretentious little village is a tribute to our heritage. Many millions of dollars and over forty years of work have gone into its meticulous reconstruction. It is, in all probablity, the most authentic restoration of a historic community that can be found anywhere in the country. Williamsburg was the capital of Virginia from 1699 to 1780. The state capitol was then moved to Richmond and Williamsburg went into a decline that lasted for almost one hundred and fifty years. In 1926, a local rector was successful in arousing John D. Rockefeller's interest in Williamsburg's spirited past. Scores of archeologists, historians, scholars, architects, and engineers were hired to recreate the Williamsburg of 1780. A detailed plan was drawn up for the preservation and restoration of the surviving buildings, of which there were approximately eighty, and for fifty additional structures to be rebuilt on their original sites, complete with streets, gardens, and authentically furnished interiors. In Williamsburg today, over twenty craft shops demonstrate the skills that were prevalent two hundred years ago. Cars are banned on the streets during the daytime as carriages and oxcarts make their way through the town to the mill where flour is ground, to the baker whose only tools for baking are a hearth and a fire, to the silversmiths, the cobblers, or perhaps the candlemakers. Compare all of this with the hustle and bustle of our own lives. No wonder so many of us suffer from heart disease, hypertension, ulcers, colitus, arthritis, to name just a few of our present day social diseases of the mind, body, and spirit.

Life does not have to be the rat race that we have turned it into; it can be a source of peace and joy. We will have to make a few adjustments but in the end, it will be well worth the compromise. To once again be able to walk down the street without fear of an assault will in itself be a blessing. To live free of the fear of a nuclear attack will give us hope for the future. We live with so many fears we are afraid of continuing inflation, a possible recession, or another depression. This is the basic difference between our lives and the lives of those who settled this land a little over two hundred years ago. They had their problems, their wars, their heartaches, but they did not endure the gnawing fear that prevails in our society today. They had hope for the future once they overcame the obstacles that confronted them. We have lost that hope. Without hope, the will to survive is depleted; without a will to live, all is lost. The only course we see left to us is to eat, drink and be merry, for tomorrow may never come. We must stop all this foolishness and forget about the moon, the x-rated movies, the discoteques, the drug trips to nowhere, and take the necessary steps backward in time in order to once again live the simple life, the quiet life, the peaceful life.

Many of us are tempted, as another birthday rolls around, to start counting backwards. We liked the years we left behind; we are not sure about the years ahead. The past had its pitfalls, but it also had its advantages. We do not know what the future holds in store, although we have a pretty good idea if things continue on as they have been. So why not opt for the lesser of two evils and put our trust and hope in reviving the past. Hindsight is greater than foresight; we can easily correct the errors made by previous generations. It will be like reliving our lives, only this time we will have all the knowledge that we have gained over the years. "If I could only live my life over again, knowing all that I know now", has been every man's wish. We can now make this dream a reality as we turn back the clock and set ourselves in a different timeframe in the development of this nation.

Extolling the virtue of the past does not reflect on our ability to maintain ourselves in a manner that is in keeping with man's original purpose to enjoy life on this planet free from want and need. It does, however, give us some idea of how things should be done. Perception of events after they have happened is a very useful tool. What once was is beginning to look pretty good; what will be depends on our willingness to take advantage of the lessons learned by studying the ways of our ancestors. The ever-increasing dilemma with which we are now faced is not, necessarily, a permanent state. It can be reversed and man can once again live life as it was meant to be. It will be up to each individual to recreate for himself some of the living conditions that were prevalent in bygone days. We can begin to heat our homes with coal or wood; we can wear clothing made from cotton, silk, or wool; we can prepare all of our foods at home and cease to rely on pre-packaged goods. The latter may take a little more time but our meals will have a greater nutritional value and be less costly. With all of our modern appliances, food preparation has been greatly simplified; chopping, mixing, and beating are now done with the push of a button. We will never again have to work as hard as our forefathers; we can enjoy the best of both worlds if we are willing to accept a compromise.

Always advancing is not what life is all about; nor is stagnation the key to successful living. It is, instead, the ability to combine the knowledge of the past with the pursuits of the present to bring about a harmonious and equitable existence for all of our fellow men. Each generation must build on what has come before; they must not tear down and try to remake the world into something that they consider better. We lose sight of our heritage and our country's history when we demolish old buildings in order to build modern edifices. We should take pride in the accomplishments of those who came before us and endeavor to restore these old structures. There is a limit as to how far civilization can go so why press our luck any farther? Why not just stop in our efforts to forge ahead and settle for a combination of the past and the present as a way to stabilize the future?

The "grass is always greener" and the lights always look brighter somewhere else, until we take a closer look and discover that there really isn't any difference. It is just wishful thinking on our parts. We may as well accept what we have and forget about our pipedreams of a twenty-first century when cities will be built in the air, visits to the Moon will be routine, all food will be consumed in a capsule form, robots will do all of our chores, and we will all have Superman's extraordinary powers. Let us accept the reality of our situation and begin to enjoy what we do have. Take the time to look at the wonders of the natural world around you, start a garden, enjoy a craft, take a walk, sit under a tree, do something that will bring peace to your soul. Nobody is making you be involved in all of the "far-out" happenings of these times. It may be easier to journey back into the past than it will be to fight your way in the future.

Chapter Eighteen
Our Space In The Universe

When the earth was created, it was given to man as his space in the Universe. Other planets were created but what their purpose is in the overall scheme of things is not for us to concern ourselves with discovering. We have our work cut out for us right here and we have no reason to infringe on the territorial domain of whomever or whatever may exist elsewhere in the Universe. Everything has a purpose and a reason for being, but it is not for us to determine the mystery that lies behind the Creation. We can enjoy the warmth of the Sun, the light of the Moon, and the twinkling of the stars since this was obviously meant to be. But just as we caution little children as they watch in wonder as a fire blazes, we may look but we may not touch for we, too, might very easily be burned. What is out there in the unknown must remain, for us, unknown. Nowhere in the teachings offered to us as a guide for living have we been told to explore the heavens above. We would be wise to adopt a policy of isolation that relates not only to other countries but also to other planets and to learn to be grateful for what we have been given to enjoy.

To truly appreciate the wonders of the world as it exists in its natural state is to know that the Creator had our best interest at heart.

There is so much in nature that some people never see. They are locked into areas comprised of concrete, brick, and mortar that have replaced the grass, the wild flowers, and the trees. It is a sad state when individuals go through life without ever having an opportunity to know the true beauty that abounds where man-made cities have not yet been built. What a waste of a lifetime!

Everyone needs a place that he can call his own. It may be a tent, a teepee, a houseboat, a trailer, an apartment, a simple house, or a glorious mansion; whatever suits an individual's lifestyle and pocketbook. Be it ever so humble, so grand, so old, or so new, we must all find a haven that is our very own; our space on this vast expanse of this planet. We may share our domain with family members or friends, or we may occupy it alone. For the most part, people choose to live in a geographical area that is inhabited by others with the same cultural or ethnic background; this makes for a more compatible and harmonious existence as we all enjoy the company of our peers. To isolate oneself from his fellow man is a very unnatural condition. We need the companionship of others in order to develop interpersonal relationships, to test our own ability, to develop a sense of being necessary for another's welfare, to understand that others are concerned about us, and to learn the value of love. These experiences are essential to the total development of a personality. As we observe all of the wildlife in nature, we can see that they never live segregated from other members of their species; it is not a natural state of being. To be a hermit garbed in a loincloth and living in a cave may, at times, seem to be the solution to all of man's problems, but it is not to be truly alive. It is the give and take of everyday living situations that develops one's values and teaches patience, tolerance, and understanding of the ways of others. We must learn to live with individual differences and to appreciate the need to share our unique talents in order to have an opportunity to benefit from all the human resources that are available. Each of us has the potential to contribute to the growth and development of other individuals.

Once we understand that we have been granted the use of a space on the Earth in which to live out our lives, we will appreciate the need to properly care for what we have been given. It is as if we were to allow a friend the use of our home while we were absent for an extended period of time. Upon our return we would expect to find things as we left them, or some improvements made as a way of showing appreciation for our generosity. And so it should be with that which we have to use as we spend our lifetime as a guest of the Creator of this planet. We should think of ourselves as being on a vacation that we hope to enjoy, and act as we would if we had made reservations to stay at a resort or hotel of our own choosing. When we are on a holiday, we do not attempt to rearrange the facilities to suit our every whim; we generally try to abide by the established practices and to adjust to the accommodations. We also make an effort to leave our vacation spot in pretty much the same state as we found it to be in on our arrival. If we are responsible for any damages, we understand that we are expected to make amends. This is how we should treat our stay on this planet; there will always be someone coming along after us to use the same facilities and it would be a kind gesture to leave everything in good repair. If each and everyone of us would adopt such an attitude and then follow through in our actions, the space we occupy would be a place of beauty and a joy to visit. The good that we do will live after us but, unfortunately, so will the devastation and destruction.

To have respect for one's own property is very important; to respect the property of others is equally important. We do not want our space invaded without our consent, therefore, we should show the same consideration to others. We have no right to trespass. However, there are areas such as public parks and beaches that we may use without being granted permission. They do not belong to any one individual and are either government sponsored, state owned, or a community project. A fee may be charged in order to maintain these recreational areas, but admission must not be denied to anyone because of race, creed, or color. We do have laws that prohibit discrimination but, unfortunately, they are all too often ignored. Each individual using such facilities must be responsible for his own conduct and adhere to the established rules and regulations. Failure to do so should result in the offending person being barred from the premises for as long a period of time as is deemed necessary by those in a position of authority.

Hunting and fishing in regions designated for these purposes should be regulated as to the times for such activities to take place and a limit set on the number of wildlife that can be removed. No man should hunt or fish for more than his family and friends can consume; to do so, just for the sport of killing, is not to be tolerated.

We think of the Earth as belonging to mankind alone, but we would not survive without the wildlife and the vegetation that is part of the whole scheme of things. For this reason we must consider the rights of all that abound in nature when it comes to allocating space on the Earth plane. It is far more important to provide areas for the growth and development of our natural resources than it is to build vast structures to house our ever-increasing technological experiments into the unknown. We know what is here for us to utilize for our own survival, why don't we just count our blessings and leave well enough alone? We would then have no need for such useless endeavors as the manufacture of synthetic foodstuffs in order to compensate for what we have destroyed in the natural world around us.

Artificial foods are now being produced that contain no vitamins, minerals, or energy-producing calories. They fool us into thinking that we have eaten a substantial meal as they easily appease the appetite, however, we could actually be starving to death on a full stomach. One of the materials used in producing synthetic foods is cellulose, which is also used to manufacture rayon and cellophane. While we are enjoying some gastronomical feast, we may actually be eating a piece of a tree. Logs are split and treated with chemicals to make wood pulp from which cellulose is obtained. The cellulose used for food is then purified and converted into a gel or a fine flour for making a variety of foodstuffs; e.g., cookies, ice cream, whipped cream, candy, cheesecake, cheese dips, mayonnaise, salad dressings, hollandaise sauce, spaghetti, or potato pancakes. Artificial foods are slowly but surely replacing those found in nature and our dream of living on a pill, rather than three meals a day, no longer seems to be beyond our grasp. Still this will never lead to a happy, healthy, well-fed nation of people.

Our ultimate goal should be to have our space in the Universe restored to a state of national pride. Suppose we were to have visitors from another planet, wouldn't we be embarrassed to have them find our homeland in such disrepair and in such an abused condition? We should even be ashamed when visitors from foreign lands visit our well-known cities. We have no right to let our metropolitan areas deteriorate into slums; it is totally unnecessary. Anyone viewing the condition of New York City would certainly never invite any of its residents to move into their geographical area; nor would they be interested in relocating in what might very aptly be called "Sin City". "The Big Apple" and "I Love New York" are fine Madison Avenue public relations slogans, but they do nothing to overcome the squalor of the South Bronx, Harlem, or a vast portion of the Borough of Brooklyn. It is truly disheartening to see what is happening to what once was an exciting and beautiful city. Mr. Carter and Mr. Reagan promised help for the South Bronx, but promises that are unfulfilled do not promote the well-being of the people who reside in the area. Action is what is needed.

It is time for a good housecleaning; communities should band together to refurbish their immediate locale. This will be a monumental task for some of the slum areas of our cities. For the residents of these devastated neighborhoods, it will have to be a block project; that is all that any group of people can be expected to deal with in a given time frame. A meeting of the residents of each block should be held to elect a block chairman who will be their spokesman as they plan for the improvement of their space. Anyone who does not cooperate should be shunned by his neighbors. This will, no doubt, cause him to leave the area or fall in line with the rest of the group. Regular meetings of the neighborhood people will be necessary to record progress, make contingency plans, and to requisition needed supplies. The city fathers should be willing to undertake the demolition of buildings that are abandoned and to replace them with park areas, recreational facilities, or make the space available to local residents for planting vegetable gardens and fruit trees. We must instill pride and hope in the people of the ghetto areas of our nation. They should be given an opportunity to become the owners of their own space. Obviously, their present landlords are not doing anything to make their tenant's living conditions tolerable and would, in all probability, be happy to accept a small sum of money for their dilapidated buildings. Government funds could be utilized to purchase these facilities which could then be offered to the present occupants, or future tenants, for a very nominal sum. Building and repair supplies could also be made available for a small fee. An "open house" should be planned by the residents of each block so that their efforts might be viewed by their neighbors. Prizes, in the form of useful household items, should be awarded to those who have been most innovative in their endeavors to refurbish their space. Joy in accomplishment, hope for a better way of life and a sense of belonging can turn a ghetto area into a place of community pride.

In Philadelphia there is one block of restored houses that can set an example for all to follow. Elfreth's Alley is a cobbled street only six feet wide that dates back to 1690. It is the oldest continually occupied street in the United States. It consists of thirty-three unpretentious homes, some of which are occupied by the descendents of the original owners. The little street was named for a blacksmith, Jeremiah Elfreth, and was often threatened with demolition. However, because of the interest of people who took pride in their heritage, it is today a perfectly restored area that is the pride of the residents as well as the city fathers. Block by block may seem like an endless process but it can be the hope for the future of our cities.

There are those who will say that we have tried to help the less fortunate members of our society by the construction of housing projects for low income families and they just did not take care of the facilities that were made available to them. Therefore, why bother to try again? Poor people will never appreciate what is done in their behalf. In some cases this is true; in others it is not. Nor do all well-to-do people take care of their homes. Many are just more fortunate in being able to pay someone to do the household and garden chores for them. They also have the funds to replace worn out or damaged items. Left to their own devices and without money for more than the bare necessities, they might not fare any better in their housekeeping than some of our indigent citizens.

We are all inclined to take better care of what is ours and what has been acquired as a result of our own efforts rather than something that has been handed to us with a few strings attached as to how we are to use and care for this contribution to our well-being. The poorest of people will take pride in ownership, in being able to better themselves, and in commanding respect for their achievements. Given a chance, a majority of the less fortunate members of our society will rise up and become solid citizens of whom we can be proud. Instead of "putting down" the unfortunate victims of our slum areas, let us help them to overcome their situation. We can lobby on their behalf to have state and federal monies allocated to their cause; not to build buildings such as housing projects, but rather to allow them to select their place of residence and refurbish it to their liking. It can be a matching-fund arrangement with the government putting up seventy-five percent of the money needed and the individuals involved in the project putting up twenty-five percent. If prices are kept within reasonable bounds, there will be no great outlay of monies on anyone's part.

We have so much to be thankful for, so much to be grateful for, and still we are not satisfied with our lot. Suppose all were taken from us and we had no place to "hang our hats". You might try to imagine what it would be like to live on a desert where the Sun never shone, the Moon never rose, the stars and the other heavenly bodies were not within your range of vision, no wildlife or vegetation abounded, and the waters of the Earth were not within your grasp. Then you would have a reason to complain about your circumstances for there would be no joy in living. This is what may someday happen to our space and if we are so unfortunate as to still be alive, these are the conditions under which we may find ourselves trying to exist. Before we take further measures to reach such an unhappy state, let us all reconsider our actions and reassess our priorities so as to make the care and nurturing of our planet our number one concern. Without this space, the human race will fade into oblivion. Without the abundance of our natural resources, all will become as a desert – devoid of the life-sustaining forces that will enable us to continue to exist. We, in essence, will be evicted from our allotted space and there will be nowhere for us to go. We may consider making reservations for accommodations on the Moon, but we cannot be certain that adequate food and lodging will be available to meet our needs. We had best repair, refurbish, and renew what we have here; there does not seem to be any other choice.

Chapter Nineteen
International Good Will

Once there is no longer a worldwide shortage of mankind's basic needs and we come to terms with the idea that what is here on Earth is for all to share, we can begin to live in peace with other nations. As we accept the premise that the Earth belongs to no man, but is just loaned to us for our use during our stay here, there will be no reason to become involved in aggressive actions to fight over what is not ours. We will, instead, realize the need to care for and preserve our own allotted space. It was this lack of understanding of our relationship with the environment that led us to create the atom bomb in the first instance. Had we been spending our time making our country a haven for its inhabitants, we would not have gotten so far off the track. What is done, is done. We will never forget our ability to destroy all mankind but we would be wise to set aside these horrendous ideas and replace them with more humanitarian goals. The right to life, liberty and the pursuit of happiness should be kept foremost in our minds as we contemplate the next decade.

International good will will not become a reality for us until we call a halt to our intervention into the affairs of other nations. Those whom we assist feel no appreciation for what we contribute. Of course they accept our handouts, but that does not mean that they, in turn, are any less hostile towards us. They see us as a soft touch and nothing more. Generally speaking, they misuse what we so foolishly send their way. It is not as if they worked hard for these things and had pride in their acquisition. If that were the case, they would be more careful in their distribution and utilization. Instead, it is just a case of easy come, easy go. The situation would also be different if countries were required to pay for, or barter for, the commodities we ship them. They would then have a vested interest in attaining what they deemed necessary for their ongoing welfare and a measure of self-esteem would be restored in their dealings with our government. They would no longer feel like a poor relation but rather as an equal.

Every nation has something that they can offer to us in payment for goods and services rendered. However, we must cease to put a dollar value on these commodities and settle for an exchange based on ability to pay, or acceptance of those resources native to the country with whom we are dealing. We must limit all of our international trade to things that are vital to the health and well-being of the populace. Under no circumstances should we be involved in supplying any type of armaments or equipment that can be used for purposes of an assault on another country. Those with whom we are doing business may send good will our way, but those who are under attack, as a result of our supplies, will not have any great love for our country.

There is so much that nations can share in order to bring about an understanding of their individual cultures. Such an exchange can truly be a way of developing an appreciation of each other's uniqueness. Every culture is different and, therefore, has its own means of expression when it comes to art, dance, and music. Unfortunately, our desire to be politically involved in the affairs of other countries keeps more away than are willing to participate in this kind of experience. Still we have had some very fine exhibitions of this type that attracted throngs of people all across the country.

When Catherine the Great was the Empress of Russia, she set out to fill a palace in St. Petersburg (now Leningrad) with Europe's finest paintings and artifacts. The result is now known as the State Hermitage Museum and it houses one of the world's finest collections. The Soviets had been reluctant to lend their treasures but in 1973, a first showing of Hermitage paintings, all French impressionist and post impressionist works, was sent to the United States. Two years later, thirty more paintings, more widely representative of European art, were exhibited at the National Gallery of Art in Washington, D.C., and from there traveled to New York, Detroit, Los Angeles, and Houston. Paintings by Rembrandt, Chardin, Gainsborough, Caravaggiocira, Guardi, Boucher, and Ruisdael, never before seen in our country, were included, as well as thirteen Russian paintings. It was a superb sampling of art.

The exhibit of three hundred and eighty-five artifacts from the People's Republic of China toured the United States in 1974. These archeological discoveries had all been unearthed since 1949 and spanned 600,000 years of Chinese cultural development. Many were of incomparable beauty and ranged from a 400,000 year old stone hammer to frail fourteenth century porcelains. Archeologists who catalogued the exhibit in Peking gave credit to the working class for many of the technical advances of ancient times; e.g., making paper, improving methods for manufacturing iron tools, brocading silk, and using acupuncture needles of gold and silver. It was a rare privilege for the American people to have an opportunity to view these national treasures of China's past.

In 1977, the King Tut exhibit of the findings that resulted from diggings into the Valley of Kings in Egypt arrived in America for a two and one half year tour. Fifty-five of the tomb's most magnificent treasures were sent by ship; twenty had never before been outside of Egypt. Each major object was packed and boxed separately and then rope-tied to a grilled metal deck so that it would not shift or shake loose. Two ships of the United States Sixth Fleet, the Milwaukee and the Sylvania, transported the precious cargo in the course of a normal rotation home.

Tutankhaman, Pharaoh of Egypt from 1334 to 1325 B.C., lived during a era of extraordinary wealth and power. The artists of the day worked in gold, silver, alabaster, obsidian, lapis lazuli, wood, glass, and gems. When he died at the age of eighteen, after a nine year reign, his tomb was crammed with objects to ease his life in the afterworld. King Tut's tomb remained inviolate until 1922 when British archeologist Howard Carter and his sponsor, Lord Carnarvon, discovered it. The splendors that they found electrified the world. The contents of the tomb, full of clues to Egyptian history and the Egyptian way of life, revealed to our twentieth century eyes the magnificence of this ancient culture.

What better way is there to develop a true appreciation of the human greatness of those of other nations than to promote such exchanges of the heritage and brilliance of their people?

As we come to the realization that all men throughout the ages have been equal to us in their capabilities and that we are no better just because we live in what we think of as "the land of the free", we will understand why we have no right to look down on others or consider them inferior. We are not the first to have adopted this attitude; there have always been groups of people and even nations who have set themselves up as being superior to the rest of the world. An example of this is found in the practice of slavery, which has been with us for as long as we are able to delve back into the history of man. It has not been one of mankind's greatest achievements; rather it has taken its toll and left bitter feelings between races of people and nations. Amends must now be made for these past errors and respect and equality granted to all the people of the earth.

Black may not be beautiful to the white people, but it is beautiful to those whose skin color reflects their African heritage. The Orientals, with their small stature and slanted eyes, have a charm that is uniquely theirs. And so it is with all the different cultures, each in its own way is very special. We must begin to regard these varying characteristics of national origin as we do the different varieties of flowers, trees, birds, animals, fish and insects that we find in nature; each has its own beauty and serves a purpose in the overall scheme of things. One cannot survive without the other. The same holds true for the human race; no one culture can expect to dominate the world as each has a role to play that cannot be usurped by others. Different nationalities thrive in different climates and understand the terrain that they inhabit. In essence, it is their God-given right to be where they are by virtue of their own ability to deal with their situation. Those who live in the tropics would not survive under artic conditions. Ice fishing is a way of life for the Eskimos; it would be totally beyond the capabilities of the natives of Barbados who grow sugar cane.

Once we understand that there is an overall plan for the care and maintenance of this planet and that our area of concern is limited to our own country, we will cease to try to force others into our mold. We will see the need to allow each individual country, race, or culture to live in accord with what has been granted to them as their area of responsibility. Some will be in a leadership role; others will be involved in industrial pursuits; still others will develop land; many will be ministers of healing and will seek to discover the medicines inherent in nature; some will hunt and fish; while others probe the Earth for its natural resources. Each will explore their own terrain and care for and nourish that which is available to them for their own survival. Who are we to tell others how to cultivate their land, how to dress, and what lifestyle would be best for them to adopt. Their customs have been handed down to them by their forefathers and, no doubt, represent the best way to survive in their geographical area. Once we learn to have respect for the ways of those who choose to live in a manner that differs from ours, we will begin to experience a sense of tolerance and an understanding of the need for all to do what is best for themselves, not what is best for us.

With tolerance and understanding comes good will. They go hand in hand in all areas of life; it is almost as if "you can't have one without the other". As a practice, they are a lot less time consuming and less expensive than the measures we have been using in our efforts to achieve the same result. Obviously, we have been taking the wrong approach; no wonder we have not been meeting with any success. What can we do to remedy the situation? We might start by putting an end to foreign aid with strings attached, by adopting an attitude of peaceful co-existence, and by showing respect for the rights of others to live as they choose. In essence, we can sit back and do nothing other than mind our own business. Should we be asked to support some project or to become involved in an exchange of ideas, we can then let our point of view be made known and accept or decline the offer to be involved, depending on our interest in the proposal. We need not be at the mercy of every country that asks for our assistance. They may have to shop around elsewhere to find a buyer for their plan. As a nation, we have a right to choose our area of involvement without others telling us what we must support. Patience and tolerance must flow in both directions.

We have no need to send ambassadors of good will all over the world to establish diplomatic relationships; nor do we need summit meetings to determine future policies. Our involvement in covert activities is of little or no value. In most intances, it is used as a cover for our own meddling in the affairs of other nations or to conceal some blunder made by our foreign policy advisors. All of these practices are an unnecessary waste of the taxpayer's money. We may want to send a representative to a very special occasion, such as the coronation of a king or a queen, the funeral of a head of state, or to a royal wedding. Such a gesture will aid in promoting good will. We might use as a guideline for our participatin in the affairs of other countries the receiving of an invitation to be present at such an event. We will be a welcome guest as long as we abide by the rules of behavior established by the host country. We expect dignitaries from foreign nations to adhere to our accepted standards, therefore, we should have little difficulty in understanding why we should abide by theirs. "What is sauce for the goose, is sauce for the gander", wherever we may roam. Our representatives must also be cautioned not to express their ideas or opinions unless they are requested. To do so may be the cause of our name being removed from the guest list for future events.

The "Ugly American" does not score points for his country. He would be better off remaining at home. Any time American citizens travel abroad, they create an impression that reflects on our nation as a whole. Much ill will has been caused by individuals who were overbearing, condescending, and oblivious to the right of those whose homeland they were visiting. Should you find yourself in the role of a tourist, act as if you are in the home of a very important person upon whom you want to make a favorable impression. First impressions may not be lasting, but when that is all one has to go by, they do leave their mark. It is always advisable to study the customs of the country and its people before embarking on a trip to a foreign destination. The more informed you are, the more you will enjoy yourself as you will be treated with the same respect that you afford to the natives of the area that you are visiting. They will be happy to share their local color with you once they know that you are interested and appreciative of their efforts. A sincere "thank you" on your part is all it will take to leave behind a feeling of respect for all Americans.

Long before our country was established, fighting existed between nations; it continues to this day. We cannot stop it by force, aid or intervention. However, we may be able to join forces with all other nations to embark on a plan to establish international peace. It could be our gift to humanity. With this as our ultimate goal, let us abolish all negative thoughts from our minds and develop a positive attitude toward those who do not share our heritage. Let us think of them as our brothers and sisters, aunts and uncles, grandmothers and grandfathers – all members of one big family that comprises the human race. As we are able to resolve differences in our individual family units through patience, tolerance and understanding of each person's rights, so let it be with the entire world population.

Our greatest hope is for the establishment of a World Council (See Chapter VI) with representatives from every nation, to deal with issues of international concern; e.g., peaceful co-existence, distribution of natural resources, aid in time of natural disaster, etc. The United Nations headquarters is located in our own country, in New York City, and, therefore, we are in a position to make overtures to expand its powers to deal with these concerns. This will not be an easy task, but it is not impossible. We already have a start in that we have a building large enough to house all of the delegates. A proposal for such action would have to initiate in Washington, D.C. and have the approval of both Congress and the President. It would then be a matter of our representative to the United Nations presenting it to the General Assembly for their consideration. Once the mechanics are put into motion, we will at least be started on the right track. How long it will take for such a measure to be approved by the present members of the United Nations is an unknown factor. However, without a beginning, there can be no conclusion. Enough of the world powers should be willing to take a strong stand in favor of such a motion. They are experiencing the same international problems as we are; some are in even more immediate distress. We need do no more than make a proposal to have a committee formed, with representatives from different cultures and different areas of the world, to draw up a tentative schedule for dealing with existing international problems. Defining the areas for consideration would be the first order of business; accepting these issues as being of major concern to all the delegates would follow. The matters to be acted on could then be dealt with on a priority basis. Acceptance of the solutions, as presented, would, undoubtedly, be the biggest obstacle to overcome. Certainly not all are going to be in accord with what is proposed, but success in any one area would be a major breakthrough and serve as a catalyst to continue to forge ahead.

"Peace on earth good will to all mankind" should be our goal.

The only way that we as a nation can be instrumental in bringing this to fruition will be by the example that we set of adapting a policy of isolationism. Once other countries realize that we are no longer going to infringe on their rights to conduct their affairs in the manner of their choosing, they will cease to look to us for assistance and begin to assume responsibility for their own people and their territorial domain. In all probability, it will take the voice of the vast majority of our people to influence those in a position of authority to initiate the action necessary to put an end to our involvement in the affairs of other nations for anything other than an exchange of resources and cultural accomplishments. The silent minority will never bring peace to mankind. They will only permit the continuation of the self-destruct policies that are now in effect. They may feel that they are unable to do anything to change existing conditions and they will be correct in their assumption as long as they continue in their passive role.

We must inform our elected officials of our desire to cease to be responsible for those of other nations, that our concerns are solely for our own people and our own homeland. We should ask for a cut in defense spending and a reduction in the size of the armed forces, as our only need in this area is to provide for the safety of our country against an attack on its territorial domain by land, sea, or air. The role that you are being asked to assume is not difficult, it is within the capabilities of all of our citizens. Do not underestimate your own importance, you cannot change the world on your own but you can be a contributing factor. If you do not feel confident to act alone, call upon a group of your associates to draft a letter with reference to these objectives. It can then be signed by all who are instrumental in its inception, or copied and mailed on an individual basis. However you choose to deal with the issue, it is important to remember that we cannot expect to overcome the ills of our time if we do not take some positive action. Too little, too late will never resolve the problem.

Chapter Twenty
Peace On Earth Good Will To All Mankind

The goal of mankind should be to restore the Earth to its original state so that all may live with an abundance of its natural resources. When this is achieved, good will shall prevail and health and happiness abound. It will be a time for rejoicing and raising our voices in thanks and appreciation for all that is once again ours to enjoy. As we reap the rewards of the completion of the task we are now embarking on – the preservation of our small space on this planet – we will know the joy of living without want or need. We will come to understand the true meaning of liberty, equality, and justice for all, for this will be the premise on which the laws of our land will be based. Our newfound well-being will surely inspire others to emulate our ways and this great country will again be looked upon with honor and respect. The final victory will be ours; not brought about by means of force, but by the love and kindness we show in our dealings with our fellow man. We will all regard with disbelief the fate to which we nearly succumbed as we dug ourselves into a hole so deep that we were almost unable to rise up again. We will never want to return to our errant ways of the past.

With the accomplishment of this goal, we will have set the wheels in motion for a lasting peace. Evil will begin to dissipate; there will be no place for it in our daily lives. Evil cannot thrive in a peaceful atmosphere, it only breeds on discontent and unrest; the good of all mankind is not its purpose. Once we are free of evil's influence, a new sense of joy will prevail. Man will no longer be at the mercy of his fellow man, the decadence that now exists will cease to plague us. We will have no need for prisons, law enforcement officers, criminal courts, or rehabilitation centers for drug addicts and alcoholics. The majority will rule and be strong enough to overcome all that has created the terror that abounds in our world today. We will be able to walk on our city streets without fear of an impending attack. The rich, the poor, the young, and the old will all be accorded the same respect as they go about their daily affairs. It will be as if our country is just one big happy family interested in the well-being of each other.

The return of an abundance of all that we require to meet our basic needs will bring with it the stabilization of prices for goods and services. Profits will reflect the overall cost of production, individual need, and a reserve for contingencies. With price gouging out of the picture, we will all be able to live with less monetary wealth, but this does not mean that we will have less of the things needed to make our lives enjoyable. Bartering for goods and services will be an accepted practice. Large companies will be prohibited from building empires and making excessive profits. They will be regulated by government controls created to ensure the greatest good for the greatest number of our countrymen. The federal government will be obliged to limit its tax structure so as to allow the people to keep most of their earnings. The only programs that will be funded out of tax dollars will be those in the areas of health, education, welfare, unemployment compensation, nutrition, food stamps, social security, assistance for the elderly, the disabled, the retarded, and environmental protection. With the elimination of foreign aid, defense spending, space travel, nuclear research, technological advancement, and bureaucratic waste of manpower and funds, we can hope to support the government with about ten percent of our earned income being allocated for tax purposes. Our whole economy will then level off and be restored to a sound fiscal state.

A government of the people, by the people, and for the people will be restored; Abraham Lincoln will not have fought in vain for this premise. Pride in our country and our heritage will be renewed. When we have righted all the wrongs in our political system, we will understand the value of democracy as a way of life that cannot be surpassed. We will never again relinquish our rights to any political party. Our leaders will be chosen for their ability to lead and to protect all that they have been given to oversee. We will be able to look up to our elected officials, to trust in their judgment, and have faith in their proficiency to deal with the programs they are empowered to administer. We will be assured that our tax dollars will be used solely for the benefit of the citizens of this nation. It will be much like depositing our money in a reputable bank, knowing that it will be wisely invested and returned to us with interest. Financial assistance will not be granted to another nation unless so ordered by a majority vote of the populace. The will of the people shall prevail!

As we come to find ourselves living in this ideal state, we will want to share our good fortune with others. We have compassion for our fellow man and do not want to see any country annihilated by their own stupidity, but we cannot use force or even friendly persuasion to aid them in their cause. We can only set an example. Delegates from all over the world come to New York City to attend the sessions of the United Nations and they are well aware of what is happening in our country; a first-hand report is available to them at all times. As conditions continue to improve on the homefront, bringing with them our personal salvation and a return to national sanity, others will take notice. Our newfound joy will become obvious and will, in all probability, spill over into other areas of the world. No leader wants his country and his people in a state of unrest and want; most will be willing to try any solution that has proven to be worthwhile. With our successes becoming more and more apparent, others will begin to seek our advice and we will then be in a position to speak of our ways for overcoming obstacles. The only advice worth giving is that which has been requested; only then will it be taken with more than a "grain of salt".

Success breeds success. Those who choose to follow in our footsteps will soon be enjoying the fruits of their own efforts. No country will want to be left behind as they see others forging ahead to a newfound way of life that is bringing peace and economic stability to its populace. With the spreading of good will throughout the world, countries will begin to ban together for the common purpose of preserving this happy state. This will be the time for a World Bank to be formulated for the distribution of goods on a fair and equitable basis to all the peoples of the world. It will also be the time for International Laws to be adopted that will enable disagreements between nations to be resolved in an impartial and peaceful manner.

There is hope for the future. There is hope for all mankind to be able to live in a state of peace and joy for all time. We can lead the way to achieving this goal; no other nation is in as good a position as we are to be the initiator of this cause. A mighty mountain lies ahead; we have the ability to surmount it if we so choose. What awaits us on the other side is an untroubled world to be enjoyed by all who follow the way and do not turn back if the going seems too hard.

Out of the darkness will come the light; so it has always been and so it will always be. For some the darkness lasts longer than for others, but the end result is always the same. This is the faith and the hope upon which we can base the future of our nation. No matter how black things may seem, if we do not give up, but see them through to the completion of our goal, we will see the light. It shines for all men, not just a chosen few; only those who cannot wait or will not make the effort that is required to overcome the obstacles the darkness confronts them with will be doomed to a fate of eventual disaster. Those of us who are willing to make the necessary sacrifices to carry on until the new day dawns will reap the rewards of our efforts and live in peace and joy for the remainder of our days. This is the promise that has been handed down to us, "The meek shall inherit the Earth". This may sound like a sermon, but a sermon according to Mr. Webster is: "a discourse delivered in public, usually by a clergyman, for the purpose of religious instruction and grounded on some text or passage of the Scripture." This does not fit the bill.

Those who follow the dictates of a particular religion believe that their "God" is the only "God" and that they are the chosen people. They fail to realize that we are all God's children with the same opportunity to live our lives in a manner that is a tribute to His greatness, or to fall by the wayside and create our own hell. There is only one way but it is for all men, not just those of a given faith, that will lead us to the Promised Land where all will live with an abundance of those things needed for their survival. To reach this destination, we must abide by the teachings of the One who is the donor of this gift to all men, for all time. If we are going to lead the way for others to follow, it is not because we are a chosen few, it is only because we have been fortunate enough to see the light and have decided to put forth the energy needed to reach our destination. Should we be the first to arrive, let us rejoice; for the good that we have accomplished will pave the way for others to share in our newfound blessings. Those who do not choose to follow in our footsteps may never live to see the error of their ways. Thus, we may be able to rid ourselves of the evil forces that have plagued mankind since the beginning of time. A noble task is ours if we care to accept the challenge. What better way is there to live out our lives than to be among those who helped to restore "Peace on Earth and Good Will to all Mankind"?

This role may seem like a monumental task; still, if we take one day at a time, it will not be so overpowering. We can all deal with today if that is all that we have to be concerned with. Therefore, as we set out to achieve our goal, let us not lose sight of our destination but let us also not try to see beyond "this" day's tasks. It would be wise to decide what area of influence you wish to tackle in your personal commitment to improving the quality of life in our country. Then each morning make a list of what you hope to accomplish in the next twenty-four hours and try to include one step toward fulfilling your chosen purpose. Do not burden yourself with unnecessary chores; to allow your energy to be dissipated in many different directions will not lead to success in any area.

It may be helpful to have a list of the concerns that must be dealt with as we forge ahead to restore our nation to a state of grace, so that you can select your point of interest. Each of us will, no doubt, align ourselves with the cause that has the greatest impact on our life. Many others will share your same goal and you should try to band together in your efforts; there is strength in numbers. We must not "spread ourselves too thin" by trying to take on more than we can handle. With the millions of people who reside in our country, we should have no trouble in having all matters of concern acted upon at the same time. Action will be needed in the following endeavors:

1. The establishment of a national health insurance program.

2. To provide all employed and self-employed persons with benefits as follows: health insurance, vacations, unemployment compensation, and a financial plan for retirement.

3. To ensure all of our countrymen their right to life, liberty, and the pursuit of happiness.

4. To provide a decent wage for all of our working force that, for the most part, will be theirs to use for their own purposes.

5. To establish price controls for all business and industry that allow for a margin of profit in keeping with manufacturing costs, overhead, and a reserve for contingencies.

6. To establish a system for bartering of goods and services.

7. To provide for the continuance and supervision of social programs relating to: unemployment compensation; food stamps; welfare payments; nutrition programs; medicare; social security; housing for the elderly; the care, education, and housing for the retarded; and assistance as needed for the disabled..

8. The establishment of an unarmed army of American youth for the purpose of improving the environment and the quality of life of our indigent citizens.

9. The elimination of defense spending for anything other than the equipment necessary to protect our territorial boundaries from attack by land, sea, or air.

10. The termination of all nuclear production of arms and

ammunition, as well as the elimination of the present stockpile.

11. The termination of all space travel.

12. The termination of all nuclear and technological research.

13. To embrace moderation in all areas of our lives and cease to pursue material goods, monetary wealth, and mind-boggling forms of entertainment.

14. The elimination of unnecessary manpower, waste of supplies, and excessive spending in the bureaucracies of our local, state, and national governments.

15. To reduce the number of agencies and bureaus under the jurisdiction of the federal government.

16. To eliminate any local or state agencies that duplicate services, or do not function in accord with their designated purposes.

17. The elimination of aid, of any nature, to foreign countries unless it is approved by a majority vote of the populace.

18. To establish stricter laws for dealing with criminals with a fixed sentence for all convicted of the same crime.

19. To eliminate bail and parole for those sentenced to a prison term.

20. To establish a fee for food and lodging for all those who are incarcerated.

21. To legalize drugs and establish controls for their sale in the same manner as we now control the sale of alcoholic beverages.

22. To eliminate alcohol and drug rehabilitation centers for adults.

23. To continue the revenue sharing program in order to enable individual states to provide public transportation and to assist their cities, as needed, in providing essential services, summer employment for high school and college

students, and to finance the redevelopment of slum areas.

24. The preparation of job descriptions for all elected officials.

25. The establishment of a policy requiring performance evaluations for all of our elected officials.

26. To reduce the amount of money allocated for expenses incurred by our elected officials.

27. The presentation of the federal budget for approval by the populace.

28. The presentation of individual state budgets for approval by the people who reside within their territorial boundaries.

29. To limit the federal income tax to ten percent of an individual's earned income.

30. The elimination of taxes on all monies that have already been taxed.

31. The elimination of all state sales and income taxes.

32. The elimination of government control of the crop output of farmers.

33. To become self-sufficient in our own communities, and in our country as a whole.

34. To provide for the protection of our environment and its wildlife.

35. To show respect for the land and to return it, wherever possible, to its natural state and its intended use: to supply all of its inhabitants with their basic needs.

36. To put an end forever to our vast waste of our natural resources.

37. To return to the good life, the simple life, and to enjoy the natural wonders of the world around us.

38. The establishment of a government of the people, by the

people, and for the people.

39. And last, but not least, to accept the teachings of the ancient prophets who were chosen by the Creator to provide us with a guide for living on this planet, as well as the acceptance of a Supreme Being as the guiding force and protector of all that is.

Here we have a thirty-nine point plan that can lead us to the achievement of our goal. It is the way for our country to renew itself and its people. There are so many areas that need to be dealt with before the end of this century, surely there must be something that will be of interest to each and everyone of us as we begin to chart our course for the future. The concern that you choose is not as important as is your willingness to become involved and to start today on the path that leads to a lasting peace on earth for all time. The holocaust can be avoided. The annihilation of the planet on which we live need not come to pass. The human race shall not perish from the Earth. Together we can forge ahead and pave the way to a life where truth and beauty, peace and wisdom, and hope for the future of mankind will prevail. THERE IS A WAY.

Bibliography

Adler, Irving. ***Petroleum, Gas, Oil and Asphalt***. The John Day Company, New York, 1975.

Bowman, John S. ***The Quest for Atlantis***. Doubleday and Co., Inc., New York, 1971.

Brant, Irving. ***Impeachment: Trials and Errors***. Alfred Knopf, New York, 1972.

Cole, Mabel Cook. ***Story of Primitive Man***. University of Knowledge, Inc., 1940.

Grant, Michael. ***The Twelve Caesars***. Charles Scribners and Sons, New York, 1975.

Gregg, Charles T. ***Plague***. Charles Scribners and Sons, New York, 1978.

Hogarth, Paul. ***Walking Tours of Old Philadelphia***. Barre Publishing, Mass., 1975.

Jordan, Mildred. ***The Distelfink Country of the Pennsylvania Dutch***. Crown, New York, 1978.

Kavaler, Lucy. ***The Artificial World Around Us***. The John Day Company, New York, 1963.

Lakan, Carli. ***Serving in the Peace Corps***. Doubleday and Co., Inc., New York, 1970.

Lent, Henry B. ***The Peace Corps: Ambassadors of Goodwill***. The Westminster Press, Philadelphia, 1966.

McGuire, E. ***The Peace Corps: Kindlers of the Spark***. The Macmillan Company, New York, 1966.

Milhollen, Hirst D. ***Presidents on Parade***. The MacMillan Company, New York, 1948.

Robbin, Irving. ***Lost Cities***. Grosset and Dunlop, New York, 1962.

Rosenberg, Philip. ***The Spivey Assignment***. Holt, Rinehart, and Winston, New York, 1979.

Seeman, Bernard. ***Electricity and Magnetism***. Harvey House, New York, 1967.

Sherrill, Robert. ***Military Justice is to Justice as Military Music is to Music***. Harper and Row, New York, 1970.

Silverberg, Robert. ***Lost Cities and Vanished Civilizations.*** Chilton Company, Philadelphia, 1962.
Williamson, Harold E. and Arnold R. Daum. ***Petroleum By-Products.*** Northwestern University Press, Illinois, 1959.
Young, William H. ***Introduction to American Government.*** Appleton-Century-Crofts, New York, 1956.

Publication and Periodicals

China's Newest Treasures. ***National Geographic***, December 1974.
Basic Facts About The United Nations. ***United Nations***, 1980.
Everyman's United Nations. ***United Nations***, 1980.
Science. July 21, 1978. American Association for the Advancement of Science. "British National Health Service: It Works and They Like It, But" – pps 239-241.
Science. July 28, 1978. American Association for the Advancement of Science. "British National Health Service: The Doctor's Dilemma" – pps. 325-329.
Report of the Secretary – General Kurt Waldheim – on the Work of the Organization. ***United Nations***, 1980.
The Treasures of King Tut's Tomb. ***Readers Digest***, January 1977.
Treasures of America. The Readers Digest Association, Inc., 1979.